GREAT
BRITONS

GREAT BRITONS

NELSON by David Howarth
THOS. COOK & SON by John Pudney
FLORENCE NIGHTINGALE by Philippa Stewart
ROBERT BURNS by David Daiches
MARLBOROUGH by Correlli Barnett
LLOYD GEORGE by John Grigg

BOOK CLUB ASSOCIATES
LONDON

In the BBC1 series of the same name
the producers are Harry Hastings, Malcolm
Brown and Jonathan Stedall, with Harry
Hastings as Executive producer.

This edition published 1978 by
Book Club Associates
by arrangement with the
British Broadcasting Corporation
35 Marylebone High Street
London W1M 4AA

ISBN 0 563 172797

First Published 1978

Printed in England by
Whitstable Litho, Whitstable, Kent.

PICTURE CREDITS

CONTENTS

NELSON

DAVID HOWARTH

Any biography of Nelson should answer the question why his memory is still so revered, especially in the navy – why he has always survived the debunkers that every hero suffers from. Of course it is a matter of opinion, but probably most people who know his story well would agree: he is remembered not mainly because he was a great admiral, a great tactician, or even a great hero in the military sense – but because he was an exceptionally kind and loveable man. Not that he was a saint, far from it: he was vain, sometimes irritable, often self-pitying, and unfaithful to his wife in one tremendous love-affair. Yet somehow his very faults seem to have made the people who knew him love him all the more. No other great Briton ever won such personal devotion. When he died at Trafalgar, his fleet forgot its victory in an astonishing spontaneous outburst of grief: the commander they lost seemed much more important to them than the triumph they won.

I was born 29 September, 1758, in the parsonage-house [at the village of Burnham Thorpe in Norfolk], was sent to the high school at Norwich, and afterwards removed to North Walsham; from whence I went to sea with my uncle, Captain Maurice Suckling, in the *Raisonable* of sixty-four guns.

Nelson was a prolific writer – eight large volumes of his letters have been published, and they were only the ones that happened to survive. But that terse statement, in his only attempt at autobiography, was all he ever wrote about his childhood. It was not that he had unhappy memories

The parsonage at Burnham Thorpe, Norfolk, where Nelson was born

of it: he just did not think it would interest anyone. Historians have had to use all the scraps of information they can to fill the gap.

The Reverend Edmund Nelson was rector of the remote little parish of Burnham Thorpe, and he and his wife Catherine had eleven children. It is a total mystery what chance of heredity produced one genius in this simple country family. Their forebears were scholarly, but nothing unusual; and out of eight children who lived to grow up, seven were very ordinary people – though they always remained a closely-knit family and were fond of each other. Mrs Nelson was related to the much grander neighbouring family of Walpole; and Horatio, the rather pompous name they gave to the sixth of their children, was a Walpole family name. He does not seem to have liked it. Most of his family called him Horace, which at least had an English air, and to most other people in his later life he was simply Nelson – or, of course, Milord.

If it was a happy childhood, it was pathetically short. Nelson must have been seven when he was sent away to boarding school; and when he was nine his mother died, and his father was left to cope with the brood of children. He evidently did his best, but on a country parson's stipend he could not do much. Somebody had to go out to work. The eldest sister was apprenticed to a milliner, and then got a job in a shop. The two elder sons stayed at school; but Nelson was so impressed with his father's poverty that when he was eleven he said he felt he ought to provide for himself. He wanted to go to sea. In later life, he never said why he chose the sea; but Burnham is on the coast, and a good many of its people were fishermen. Moreover, Mrs Nelson's brother Maurice Suckling was a senior naval captain and the children had certainly heard him tell stories of his adventures. So the family asked him to take the boy as a servant. And Captain Suckling wrote: 'What has poor Horatio done, who is so weak, that he should be sent to rough it out at sea? But let him come, and the first time we go into action a cannon ball may knock off his head, and provide for him at once.'

So on New Year's Day 1771 a very forlorn little boy reported to the naval dockyard at Chatham, where his uncle's ship was lying. He was just over twelve, and small for his age – as a man, he was under five foot six – and it was a busy place full of shipwrights and sailors. At first he could not find his uncle or the ship, or anyone who could be bothered to tell him where to go or what to do. But he persevered and settled down to the life of a captain's servant.

Servant was the technical word for such boys: in fact, they were apprentice officers. It was an extremely tough life for children – living in the cockpit of a ship below the waterline, dark and damp and comfortless and cold; instantly doing whatever they were told; always able and willing to race to the masthead 170 feet above the deck; long hours of school; and the same food the sailors had. 'Indeed,' another twelve-year-old wrote at that time, 'we live on beef which has been ten or eleven years in corn and on biscuit which quite makes your throat cold in eating it owing to the maggots which are very cold when you eat them like calves-foot jelly or blomonge being very fat indeed. Indeed I do like this life very much.'

Like it or not, this was the usual way – practically the only way – to start a career as a naval officer. One of the perquisites of a captain was the right to carry thirty or forty servants on his ship's books. Some captains, beside their stewards, cooks and valets, carried superfluous men like barbers and musicians; but most made up the numbers by taking the sons of their friends to sea, and good ones took a great interest in the education of their gang of little boys. One consequence of this system was that naval officers came from a narrow social class. On the whole, they were not aristocrats – those went into the army. They were certainly not what were called the lower classes – and indeed most crews disliked the few men who were known as tarpaulin captains, those who had worked their way up from a humble beginning. Most of them were the minor landed gentry, the squires of England. It was an unfair system, with no pretence of democracy. But it did at least produce officers who had lived under naval tradition from their childhood and were intensely proud of the service.

In the first year under Captain Suckling's eye, Nelson learned to sail a boat in the estuaries of the Medway and the Thames. Francis Drake was another boy who had his first lessons there, and it is still a good place to learn: strong tides and miles of mud that are covered at high water – these are the best of teachers. 'By degrees,' he wrote later, 'I became a good pilot, and confident of myself among rocks and sands, which has many times since been of the very greatest comfort to me.'

But after that year, Suckling thought he needed more sea experience, and he sent him in a merchant ship on a cruise to the West Indies. 'If I did not improve in my education,' he wrote of that voyage, 'I returned a practical seaman.' He was nearly fourteen.

To be a hero needs more than courage and skill, it also needs luck. Nelson was lucky in Captain Suckling's training, and lucky also in the moment at which he joined the navy: a moment which, perhaps more than any other in history, offered scope to a hero. The navy had already won the dominance at sea that he was to put the final seal on. Looking back, the year 1759, the year after Nelson was born, quite clearly marks the beginning of that dominance. That year, the British won three resounding victories over the French, at Quebec, Lagos and Quiberon Bay; and after it, the British were always seeking for battle at sea, and their ancient enemies the

11

French and Spanish were always trying to avoid it. Ships had not fundamentally changed in the past two hundred years, nor had gunnery or tactics, nor had the archaic and inefficient ways that crews were raised for the ships. But the British navy without any question was the finest navy there had ever been, and it knew it was. It sailed with utter confidence in all the oceans of the world; and it had won its battles so thoroughly that it had ships and men to spare for other things than fighting – exploration, surveying and scientific research. When Nelson joined the navy, Captain Cook was away on the first of his South Sea voyages. Three years later, as a midshipman, Nelson himself was on an Arctic expedition, stuck in the ice; and a year after that he was in Ceylon and India – all this by the time he was sixteen.

In India, he very nearly died of a tropical fever and was sent home as an invalid. It is one of the oddities of Nelson's life that he was always supposed to have a weak constitution: he believed it himself. But in fact, he tried his constitution pretty hard. At the best of times, life at sea was tough, and he twice recovered from serious fevers – this at a time when the navy lost ten times as many men from fever as it lost in battle.

In April 1777, he wrote to his brother William, who was at Cambridge:

Dear Brother . . . I passed my degree as Master of Arts on the ninth instant (that is, passed the Lieutenants' examination) and received my commission on the following day for a fine Frigate of thirty-two guns. So I am now left in the world to shift for myself, which I shall hope to do, so as to bring credit to myself and friends.

To that occasion we owe the first of many portraits, painted when he was eighteen and altered four years later to give him the insignia of a captain. Looking at that youthful face, I wonder if one can still discern in it the charm and vitality that everyone saw in the boy. For at this age he already possessed the genius for friendship which I think was the greatest of his virtues. Nobody now can quite define the quality he had; but it is a fact that all the captains he served under as a boy remained his devoted friends for the rest of their lives, or his. So did scores of young men of his own age – many, like Collingwood and Troubridge, who became famous in later years under his command. He never forgot a friend, and never lost the art of making new ones.

This teen-age portrait is also worth a careful look because in many ways Nelson remained like a pleasant teen-ager all his life, impulsive, enthusiastic, generous, naïve and strangely innocent. He never quite grew up. I think this picture may show more of him than the later portraits when his face was lined by suffering and worry, and his uniform was loaded by decorations.

The 'fine frigate' he was appointed to was the *Lowestoffe*, Captain

Nelson at the age of 18, by J. F. Rigaud. The picture was altered four years later to show a captain's insignia

Locker, bound for Barbados and Jamaica; and it was there in the West Indies that he had all his early experience of command – eight years of it, in the last stages of the American War of Independence and the uneasy peace that followed it.

Nowadays, the West Indian islands are advertised as a playground for the rich, and expensive yachts lie in most of the harbours where the men-of-war lay. But strangely, nobody in the navy in those days seems to have thought the islands were beautiful. It was not a happy station. It was full of fevers. Ashore, it was a slave society, and by then Englishmen on the whole felt uneasy about the wrongs of slavery. And of course it was hot, and the navy was badly organised for living in the heat. Naval officers always appear to have worn the same uniform whatever the climate, and never to have thought of swimming as a means of keeping cool. Nelson wrote a miserable letter from English Harbour in Antigua:

I am alone in the commanding officer's house, while my ship is fitting. The moment she is habitable in my cabin, I shall fly to it, to avoid mosquitoes and melancholies. Hundreds of the former are now devouring me through all my clothes. When you see me, I shall be like an Egyptian mummy, for the heat is intolerable. I have six pails of salt water at daylight poured upon my head.

Another source of melancholy was the war. The navy did not like fighting the American colonists. Some officers even refused to do it; the only real enemies, in their view, were the ancient enemies France and Spain. But I cannot say this ever worried Nelson. Duty was always his overriding motive, and he would fight anyone his country was at war with. He was never stuck in harbour for long. What he wanted was to be out in a ship of his own, no matter how small, and most of the time he managed it, ranging with fanatic energy up to Boston and New York, and down to Trinidad and Mexico. His ships grew in size as he grew in rank. His first was a very small schooner which was a tender to the *Lowestoffe* and was named *Little Lucy* after Captain Locker's daughter. 'In this vessel,' he wrote, 'I made myself a complete pilot for all the passages through the islands on the north side of Hispaniola.' Hispaniola was the island now called Haiti, and at that time it was French; so this was the kind of adventuring off an enemy shore which he always enjoyed. The next ship, when he was commander, was the brig *Badger*. In her, he patrolled the Mosquito Coast of Honduras. And next, he was appointed captain of the frigate *Hinchinbrooke*, thirty-two guns. This was a ship with a crew of 200 men, and Nelson was still only twenty years old.

There is a glimpse of him soon after this when he had occasion to visit the *Barfleur*, the flagship of Lord Hood, and there encountered Prince William, the future King, who was a midshipman.

NELSON

The merest boy of a captain I ever beheld [the Prince wrote afterwards]; and his dress was worthy of attention, a full laced uniform, lank unpowdered hair tied in a stiff Hessian tail of extraordinary length – the old-fashioned flaps of his waistcoat added to the general quaintness – I had never seen anything like it before. My doubts were, however, removed when Lord Hood introduced me to him. There was something irresistably pleasing in his address and conversation. I found him singularly humane . . .

It almost goes without saying that the two became friends. It was odd that the Prince should use the word humane, because he himself was a young martinet. But there is no doubt that Nelson at twenty had already found the art of balancing efficiency with humanity.

This I think was the core of his naval success. Everyone knows the fearsome punishments the navy used in those days, the floggings with the cat which at worst could maim a man or even kill him, and the final deterrent at the yard-arm. But one cannot truly see these things with modern eyes. Ships in war were manned partly by volunteers, partly by men seized by the press-gangs, and partly by minor criminals sentenced to the ships instead of prison. There was an extremely tough and lawless element among them. Nobody wanted to be shipmates with a dangerous drunk, a thief, or a man who endangered them all by sleeping on watch, and the sailors knew as well as anyone that there had to be drastic punishments. During Nelson's career, the famous mutinies happened at Spithead and the Nore. The mutineers risked their lives for the things they felt they had to demand, but they did not protest about naval punishments, only about the unfair use of them. There were weak captains who took refuge behind their power to order punishments, and there may have been some sadists who took pleasure in it. But under a fair captain, the punishments protected the crew against the lawless men among them.

Nelson was a man of his time, and he was perfectly capable of ordering a flogging: he had to be. But he only did it when he believed the good of the ship, and therefore the good of the navy, demanded it: he did it fairly in accordance with the naval law and custom that everyone understood, and he balanced punishment with generous praise and thanks for jobs well done. What he demonstrated – with some of his friends, most notably Collingwood – was that the most efficient ship was run not by fear but by strictness, fairness and human sympathy. His crews responded with loyalty and devotion. When his second frigate was paid off – he was twenty-one at the time – the entire ship's company, pressed men and all, volunteered to serve with him again; and crews made similar tributes to him all his life.

That was in wartime; but his last commission in the Indies was after the

Fanny Nelson, painted at about the age of 40

War of Independence was over, and it was not so happy or successful. He was not very good as a peacetime sailor. For one thing, there were too many social occasions; and although he was sociable enough among his friends, he was shy and awkward at formal parties. And on this commission, his strict sense of duty got him into trouble and made him, for the only time in his life, an unpopular man. By winning their independence, the Americans had made themselves legally foreigners, and under British law foreigners were not allowed to trade with the colonies. The colonists in the islands wanted and needed the American trade, and all the local civil authorities were willing to shut their eyes to it, even to take part in it themselves. But not Nelson. His duty as a naval officer was to uphold the law, and he was incapable of compromising in a matter of duty. So he set himself to stop the trade, and made the local magnates so angry that in some of the islands he could not go ashore. Of course he was right, but he was probably too self-righteous.

It made him lonely and miserable; and that may have been the cause of the one important event of this dismal commission: he got married. His bride was Fanny Nisbet, who was a widow a little older than he was, with a son of five. He had begun in 1785, when he was twenty-six, to send her formal respectful letters.

My dear Fanny, With my heart filled with the purest and most tender affection do I write this . . . I daily thank God, who ordained that I should be attached to you . . . Fortune, that is, money, is the only thing I regret the want of, and that only for the sake of my affectionate Fanny . . . My whole life shall ever be devoted to make you completely happy, whatever whims may sometimes take me. We are none of us perfect, and myself probably much less so than you deserve. I am, etc., Horatio Nelson.

This was the tone of all his letters to her. They speak of affection and respect – the word love is seldom mentioned – and are totally different from the frankly passionate adoring letters he wrote to Emma Hamilton later in his life. Why then did he ask her to marry him? One can only guess at such things, but it seems that he felt his career was going wrong and he needed sympathy and moral support; perhaps he was more in love with the idea of being married than he was with Mrs Nisbet herself. She was not the first woman he had thought of: there had been a parson's daughter who turned him down, and a beautiful young person in Quebec against whom his friends felt he had to be protected. But he had been at sea since he was a child, he cannot have known much about women, and there was not much choice of eligible sympathetic ladies in the Indies. So at twenty-seven he married Fanny Nisbet. A year later, he was back with her at Burnham Thorpe where he was born – and out of a job.

In those days, captain was the highest rank a naval officer could reach by merit; after that, it was simply a matter of seniority, or waiting for older men to die. Nelson was captain at twenty, but there he stuck until he was thirty-seven. Moreover, in peacetime there were far more captains than ships, and the great majority of them were ashore, unemployed on half pay. This was Nelson's fate for five frustrating years, a strange interlude when the country had no use for him. He went back to living the aimless life of a minor country gentleman, always short of money, bored to death and longing for the sea. Poor Fanny was not a great help; it was no fault of hers, but she had no resources of character that could have helped him. After the Indies, she hated the cold and damp of the Norfolk parsonage and often spent days in bed with chronic but ill-defined complaints. She bore him no children, and that was an added misfortune because he loved children and was very good with them. She had no sympathy for his restless mind, or his passionate wish to go to sea again. But he pestered the Admiralty for another ship – any kind of ship. 'If your Lordships,' he wrote, 'shall be pleased to appoint me to a cockle boat, I shall feel grateful.'

He did not get one until he was thirty-four, in 1793, when war against France and then Spain began again. But she was a ship worth waiting for, the *Agamemnon*, sixty-four guns, his favourite of all the ships he commanded. As captain at last of a ship of the line, his genius came suddenly to flower, and he entered eleven years of excitement, adventure and growing honour and fame.

The scene of this second part of his career was mainly the Mediterranean. The navy's role was to confine the ambitions of France and especially of Napoleon within the bounds of Europe – and to keep him out of England. History credits Nelson with three devastating victories, the Nile, Copenhagen and Trafalgar. But he was first stamped a hero in the navy's eyes by the earlier Battle of Cape St Vincent in February 1797. He was serving then as commodore in the ship named *Captain*, under Admiral Sir John Jervis, when they sighted a much larger Spanish fleet off the coast of Portugal.

Until that day, the battle tactics of any fleet had been a standardised procedure. A ship's main armament could fire only within a fairly narrow arc on either beam: ahead and astern it had few guns, if any. So it was always the custom to sail into battle in line ahead, each ship protecting the stern of the one in front and the bow of the one behind. The two lines sailed on converging courses, and as each ship came in range of its opposite number it fought a duel, broadside to broadside. The only novelty had been introduced by the British, more or less by chance, within the past generation. This allowed each ship to cut through the enemy line, firing both broadsides as it went, and then haul up to attack from the other side.

When the Spanish fleet was sighted that winter's day it was not in a battle formation but in two separate groups, and Jervis took his line between them to keep them apart. Then he made the signal to tack in succession, which meant that each ship should follow his course and turn where he turned.

The line of battle had become an almost sacred institution, and it was unheard-of for a captain to leave it. But that is what Nelson did. His ship was third from the end of the line, and he saw that if he carried out the admiral's order he would be too late to take a major part in the fight. So he turned alone, wore out of line, at first away from the enemy. The other captains were aghast, it looked like cowardice, and indeed he risked his whole career. But then he bore down, still alone, on the enemy fleet and

Cape St Vincent, 1797. After the later painting by Frank Baden-Powell, this engraving shows the boarding of the San Nicolas

fought six Spanish ships one after another. He wrote a description himself of what happened:

> I was joined and most nobly supported by the *Culloden*, Captain Troubridge. The *Excellent*, Captain Collingwood, disdaining the parade of taking possession of beaten enemies, most gallantly pushed up, with every sail set, to save his old friend and messmate, who was to appearance in a critical state. The *San Nicholas* luffing up, the *San Josef* fell aboard her. My ship having lost her fore-topmast, not a sail, shroud or rope left, her wheel shot away, I directed Captain Miller to put the helm a-starboard, and calling for the boarders ordered them to board the *San Nicholas*. A soldier having broke the upper quarter-gallery window, jumped in, followed by myself and others as fast as possible. I found Captain Berry late my first lieutenant in possession of the poop, and the Spanish ensign hauling down . . . I then directed my people to board the *San Josef*, which was done in an instant, Captain Berry assisting me into the main chains. At this moment a Spanish officer looked over the quarter-deck rail and said they also surrendered. And on the quarter-deck of a Spanish first-rate, extravagant as the story may seem, did I receive the swords of vanquished Spaniards; which as I received, I gave to William Fearney, one of my barge-men, who put them with the greatest sang-froid under his arm. Thus fell these ships.

Perhaps it was a rather self-centred account, but when Nelson was proud of something he never hesitated to say so; and to balance it one must add the equally typical letter he wrote to Collingwood next day: 'My dear good Friend, "A friend in need is a friend indeed" was never more truly verified than by your most noble and gallant conduct in sparing my ship from further loss . . . ' He never forgot to say thank-you.

The navy delighted in his act of inspired disobedience (so did his admiral, luckily) and in the unique feat of boarding an enemy ship and then using that to board another. As for a commodore who would not just order a boarding party but would lead it – well, this was a crazy thing to do, but it stamped him as a man whom men would follow. For this escapade he was knighted, and by coincidence his turn came up, a few days later, to be appointed rear admiral.

It goes without saying that Nelson was a brave man – though as a matter of fact, with his oddly naïve vanity, he sometimes said it himself. But there is more to it than that. True courage is the strength of mind to overcome one's fear; and if one has no fear, one does not need such courage. Nelson simply had no fear, of pain or death. He loved danger, he could not resist it, it was like a drug that excited and exalted him; so that even as an admiral, whenever there was a fight he had to be in the thick of it. 'Difficulties and dangers,' he once wrote, 'do but increase my desire of attempting them.'

Some men are fearless only because they are stupid and lack imagination, but that was certainly not the reason in Nelson. Fearlessness may have been born in him together with his other marks of genius; or it may have been a conscious resolution. In his short autobiography, he wrote of the time when he was sixteen, sick with fever and acutely depressed because he thought his health would not stand up to naval life: 'A sudden glow of patriotism was kindled within me, and presented my King and country as my patron. My mind exulted in the idea. "Well then," I exclaimed, "I will be a hero, and confiding in Providence, I will brave every danger." ' And late in his life, when he was sailing into battle, he wrote a memorable sentence to comfort Emma: 'Remember that a brave man dies but once; a coward dies all his life.'

With this resolution and a trust in God, he could always enter battle with his mind composed, prepared to die. Sometimes he made a joke of it ('A peerage or Westminster Abbey!'). Sometimes, alone in his cabin, he knelt at his desk and wrote a prayer or expression of faith: 'Though I know neither the time nor the manner of my death, I am not at all solicitous about it because I am sure that God knows them both, and that he will not fail to support and comfort me.'

In that spirit, he never bothered to control his craving for danger, and he collected most of his wounds in fights that a senior officer should have kept out of: honourable scars that more often belonged to sailors than to admirals. He was blinded in his left eye directing guns on shore in Corsica. (There has been misunderstanding ever since about his eye. He is often portrayed with a patch on it like a pirate, but he never wore one: the eye was not disfigured. He sometimes wore a shade above his good eye to protect it from glare, as people now wear sunglasses.) When he lost his right arm, it was again in leading a landing-party, this time in an abortive attack on Teneriffe. In the manner of the time, it was cut off at once – with no anaesthetic, of course, and an ordinary saw. A week after, he wrote with his left hand to his commander-in-chief: 'A left-handed admiral will never again be considered as useful, therefore the sooner I get to a very humble cottage the better, and make room for a better man to serve the state.'

But six months later, he was back in the Mediterranean, now commanding a squadron of thirteen ships of the line, hunting for a huge fleet Napoleon was known to have assembled, and working his peculiar miracle of command. He had some wonderful captains in that squadron: many were old friends of his. The commander-in-chief in Gibraltar, who chose them, called them 'a few choice fellows'; but Nelson made them much more – what he called a 'band of brothers'.

Many people have tried to analyse the way he did it. To me, it seems to have been through a blend of genuine friendship – and all the humility and thoughtfulness which that implies – with unmistakable authority.

The battle of the Nile, 1798. The attack at sunset, showing Nelson's ship, the Vanguard, *with signals flying*

Whenever the weather was calm and the enemy quiet, captains were rowed to the flagship for dinner. Nelson was a famous host among his fellow-men, and these afternoons were cheerful parties. But he used them also to tell the captains precisely his plans for any possible situation they might find the enemy in; and in doing that, he assumed with total confidence that every captain and every crew would act bravely and wisely whatever happened. That confidence made the captains confident in themselves and in each other, and from them it spread to the smallest boy in the fleet.

Moreover, whenever he was aware of a job well done, he said so at once, and ungrudgingly. The small frigate *Penelope*, for example, fought a successful action all night against a much more powerful French ship. Captain Blackwood of the *Penelope*, as it happened, had never met Nelson. He had a right to expect some formal praise from his admiral, but this is what he got:

My dear Blackwood, Is there a sympathy which ties men together in the bonds of friendship without having a personal knowledge of each other? If so (and I believe it was so to you) I was your friend and acquaintance before I saw you. Your conduct stamps your fame beyond the reach of envy: It was like yourself – it was like the Penelope. Thanks; and say everything kind for me to your brave officers and men.

Napoleon's fleet sailed to Egypt, and Nelson's failed to intercept it; but found it at anchor in a bay at the mouth of the Nile.

The battle of the Nile has been called a masterpiece of tactics. So it was, but it might be better to call it a masterpiece of command; for the tactics were so perfectly understood that Nelson had no need to order them. The French were sighted late in the afternoon: Nelson had no chart of the bay they were in: the French admiral is said to have thought he was impregnable. Any lesser squadron would have had to pause, to form a line of battle, discuss a plan, perhaps to wait for daylight. Nelson had no need to pause. It did not matter who led his line, it did not matter that dusk was falling. 'I knew the men I had to trust to,' he said afterwards. 'I was sure each would find a hole to creep in at.' So they did. Everyone knew exactly what he would expect them to do, and they sailed straight in and did it.

It was the most complete naval victory there had ever been. Of the French line, only two ships escaped destruction; all the British were damaged but none was lost. Nelson was wounded again, this time in the head, and temporarily blinded in his one good eye. Characteristically, he thought he was dying. But he returned to his base at Naples, the dispatches going ahead that were to make him once and for all the supreme national hero. And waiting to welcome the hero in Naples were the British Minister and his wife, Sir William and Lady Hamilton.

Emma Hamilton was an enchanting and devastating person. She had many misfortunes in her life, and another after her death; for the Victorian biographers of Nelson condemned her utterly. Modern historians can afford to be more charitable. Emma was born in poverty. As a young teenager she was very beautiful. Her father had died when she was a baby, and she had a mother who was quite happy to live on her daughter's earnings. So Emma became a natural victim of an age when rich men bought and sold their mistresses. There were scandalous stories of her, served naked in pie-dishes at dinner parties and dancing on the tables to entertain her owners and their friends – and no doubt she had done such things. Her misfortune was that she had a real capacity for love. She fell deeply in love with some of the men who possessed her, and she was heartbroken when one of them, Charles Greville, sold her to his uncle to pay off some debts. She was twenty-one then, and the uncle William Hamilton was fifty-six, and he took her to Naples where he lived.

Crayon drawing of Emma Hamilton by Lawrence

Hamilton was a scholar, an amateur geologist, archeologist and collector of works of art, an exemplar of the civilised eighteenth-century man. He set himself to play the part of Pygmalion; and he educated his beautiful girl so well that she became a leading figure in the social and political life of Naples, and a confidante of the Queen. Among the wise and charming letters he wrote her, there are many bits of advice that are still well worth remembering – this, for example:

The whole art is, really, to live all the *days* of our life; and not, with anxious care, disturb the sweetest hour that life affords – which is, the present. Admire the Creator, and all his works, to us incomprehensible; do all the good you can upon earth; and take the chance of Eternity without dismay.

He lived with Emma seven years, and then was persuaded to marry her – knowing very well, as he said, that he would be 'superannuated' while she was still a young woman. When Nelson came back from the Nile, Hamilton was sixty-seven, and longing for a quiet studious life; the wounded hero was forty, and Emma was thirty-two: vital, colourful, restless, cheerful, generous and loving: growing stout it is true, but still irresistibly attractive.

Who then is to judge these three people? Given their characters, what happened was inevitable. The city of Naples exploded in a riot of welcome and hero-worship, Emma was at the centre of it, and Nelson always loved to be lionised. I have said that in some ways he never quite grew up, and when he fell in love at the age of forty he behaved like a boy in his first calf-love. He had never met a woman remotely like Emma, and he could not resist talking about her, praising her to everyone – even in letters to his wife in England. His old naval friends were upset that he was making a fool of himself, and that Emma would distract him from his duty. At first, she did. He could not drag himself away from her, and for some months he lost the sense of duty that had guided him all his life – even, some people would say, his sense of justice. So much so that the Admiralty recalled him to England, tactfully on the grounds of his health. He came back not by sea, as an admiral should, but overland through Austria and Germany, skirting dangerously round the edges of Napoleon's empire, and bringing both the Hamiltons with him.

Back in London, Nelson made an attempt to rejoin his wife, but it was hopeless and he left her: the only unkind act recorded of him. Fanny merits sympathy; she could not grasp the masculine concept of martial glory, and she was incapable of being a hero's wife. It was said her only comment on his triumph at the Nile was that he must always remember to change his socks. It may not be true, but it may be an illuminating story.

For a while it was a great scandal in London society. The cruel car-

Emma through the caricaturist's eye: Gillray, 1801

toonists of that era had a field-day, the snobbish world looked down its nose at Emma, the King turned his back on Nelson at a reception. He bought a house at Merton in Surrey, which now has disappeared in the spread of the suburbs of London; and here he lived with both the Hamiltons in a contented trio. Hamilton was still fond of Emma, and was devoted to Nelson. He had always known that Emma would seek another lover when he was old, and he was glad it was the man he most admired; he was happy to exchange her tempestuous love-making for Nelson's friendship. When he died, Nelson and Emma were both by his bed, and in his will he left to Nelson his favourite portrait of her – 'A small token of the great regard I have for his Lordship; the most virtuous, loyal and truly brave character I have ever met with. God bless him, and shame fall on those who do not say Amen.'

The affair has damaged Nelson's reputation in some historians' eyes, and nobody can deny the harm it did. But so far as I know he did not lose a single friend through it: all his friends waited patiently for him to recover, while the navy and the nation as a whole did not give a damn for its hero's private life. And one cannot deny that some good came out of it. In Emma, Nelson had found a woman who matched his fire and vitality – and to some degree his compassion and charity. He was always an intensely loving man: he would not have been complete if he had never

Emma, the ethereal beauty, as Romney saw her

experienced the passionate love that came to him so late in life – or the parental love, for Emma bore him his only children, his daughter Horatia and another christened Emma, whom he never saw because she died at a fortnight old. It is fair to say that Emma completed Nelson. Ever after, he was a man of two loves: his love of duty, honour, glory, the navy and the men he served with; and on the other hand his love of Emma. Both loves lasted until the very minute he died.

His life was coming towards its climax. He confirmed his reputation with another shattering victory, at Copenhagen in 1801; and in May 1803 he hoisted his flag in the most famous of his ships, the *Victory*, bound again for the Mediterranean.

The navy's task at that moment was easy to define but difficult to achieve. Napoleon's armies were ready at Boulogne for the invasion of England which was his greatest ambition. But they could not cross the Channel unless his fleet could win command of it, if only for a few days. The fleet was scattered in the ports of France and Spain from Toulon in the Mediterranean to Brest on the Bay of Biscay: and the navy's job was to keep them in port, or fight them if they tried to come out.

The kind of ship that Nelson commanded had a freedom and independence that disappeared with the age of steam; for a steamship needed fuel, but a sailing ship could stay at sea for years, and all she needed from the shore was water, wood for the galley fire and fresh food when she could get it. So it was that the sailing navy could watch and blockade its enemy's ports, day and night, summer and winter, with never a break. From the time he joined the *Victory*, Nelson was two years on board without ever setting foot ashore, and so was almost every one of her 850 men.

In those years, he was often ill. It seems likely it was chronic malaria from his early days in the Indies which made him miserably sick from time to time – besides being seasick, as he often was in bad weather. Worse than that, his good eye was fading, and he knew that before he was old he would be blind. But there must have been something psychosomatic about his illnesses too, because he was always worse when he was worried, and instantly better when there was something dangerous to do. Yet he was never off duty – and an admiral's duty on a distant station was unimaginably lonely: he was absolutely responsible, and if he ever asked for advice or orders from home, it would be months before he could look for an answer.

The long blockade of all Napoleon's ports in the years before Trafalgar was the greatest sustained and communal feat of seamanship there has ever been or ever will be. The watch on Brest was perhaps the hardest of all – a notoriously dangerous shore which lay to leeward in the prevailing winds, exposed to seas with a fetch of thousands of miles. No modern mariner would dare to explain exactly how the navy was able to stand off and on that coast, estimating the tidal streams and currents, constantly solving the problems of navigation and ship-handling – and not merely in one ship, but a whole fleet of them. The achievement astonished the French, who looked out every morning and saw the sails still there, and it is just as astonishing now. So is the toughness of the crews, who lived in wind and rain and spray, with neither shelter on deck nor warmth below.

Horatia, Nelson's daughter by Emma

Nelson's watch was on Toulon, where the problems were different. He did not try to keep the French in harbour: his burning wish was to lure them out and beat them. All the neighbouring coasts were hostile, with the exception of Sardinia, which was neutral but primitive. The nearest ports under British control were Malta and Gibraltar, each over six hundred miles away. So his fleet had to cure its own sick, repair its own ships and find its own provisions where it could. He took infinite pains to keep his crews healthy and as happy as they could be. He varied the cruising to give them another shore to look at, and varied each day by different kinds of training; and much of his thought and correspondence was spent in the search for tolerably healthy food. All that time, through his exertions, the fleet lived off the country. Men died of the ills they would have died of anywhere, but at the end the survivors were as fit as when they started, and there was only one man on the sick list of the *Victory*.

It was really this blockade, not battle, that destroyed Napoleon's navies. Stuck in harbour year after year, they lost the will and the skill to put to sea and fight. But for the British, it was deadly boring, and when at last in September 1805 the enemy fleets were cornered in Cadiz, everyone in the British ships off shore was fed up at the prospect of yet another winter at sea, and morale was low.

Nelson at that moment was not with them. For three weeks after those years at sea he was home at Merton with Emma, a taste of the happy home life that sailors dream of. Whenever he went to London in those weeks, crowds collected to cheer him – for the English looked to him as the only man who could save them from invasion. He loved it: he did like being a hero. He had no wish to go to sea again: the only thing that could have dragged him back was the chance of a final fight. When the news came from Cadiz, he went to Portsmouth to rejoin the *Victory*, and made a famous entry in his Journal; 'At half past ten drove from dear dear Merton where I left all which I hold dear in this world.' The crowds were so dense at Portsmouth that he embarked far down the shore, but they followed him and people knelt down to bless him as he passed.

When the *Victory* was sighted off Cadiz, the fleet was transformed. In those last weeks, Nelson showed all the qualities his reputation had grown on: clear thinking and bravery, warmth, understanding and tact, and the sudden unpremeditated kindnesses. He asked all the captains to dinner, half one night and the other half the next. The first evening was his birthday – he was forty-seven – and it turned into a birthday party. He had taken the trouble in England to collect messages and letters from his colleagues' wives, news of how their children were getting on. He listened to their troubles, took infinite pains to soothe any ruffled feelings. And he told them exactly how they were going to beat the enemy. He rebuilt their pride and confidence and re-awoke their affection, and those feelings spread at once throughout the fleet.

It was a revolutionary tactical plan that he described at those dinner parties. Nelson had a large fleet, the enemy even larger. No day was long enough, he said, to form so many in the usual line of battle. Therefore they would attack in two separate smaller lines, with a third in reserve. He would lead one, to cut through the enemy line at its centre, and Admiral Collingwood, second in command of the fleet, would lead the other to overwhelm the rearguard. So two separate battles would be fought, each with a superiority of numbers; and both would be won, he believed, before the enemy's van could turn in formation to take any part.

He wrote in the memorandum which confirmed what he had said:

Something must be left to chance, nothing is sure in a Sea Fight beyond all others. Shot will carry away the masts and yards of friends as well as foes; but I look with confidence to a Victory before the Van of the Enemy could succour their rear . . . No captain can do very wrong if he places his ship alongside that of an enemy.

The first problem was to tempt the enemy out of Cadiz. He stationed the fleet fifty miles off shore, out of sight, with frigates to watch the port and a line of ships to repeat their signals to him.

But it was Napoleon who drove the French and Spanish fleets to sea. After those years of blockade, the navy lying in Cadiz was already beaten. For lack of sea training, it was incompetent to sail in formation, let alone to fight; its more intelligent officers knew that if it met the British at sea, it was doomed to destruction. But Napoleon in those last weeks had had to give up his invasion of England because his fleets were unable to protect it; and he was so furious with his navy that he no longer cared what happened to it. He ordered it to sail, on a useless voyage back to the Mediterranean. His final order said: 'His Majesty's wish is that his admirals, captains, officers and men should not hesitate to attack equal or superior forces in battles of extermination. He counts for nothing the loss

The villa at Merton, after a drawing by Gyford

The Battle of Trafalgar, 1805, with the Victory *flying its famous signal; engraving after the painting by Turner*

of his ships, if they are lost with glory.'

With that fatally furious command, on 19 October, the fleets began to straggle out of harbour. Before they were out, the frigates' signals had been relayed to Nelson, and the *Victory* hoisted the flags: 'General chase south east.'

There followed a night and a day and another night of shadowing, suspense and manoeuvre. At 6 a.m. on the twenty-first, in the British ships, thirty-three sail of the enemy were sighted against the dawn. Nelson, seeing them at last where he had always longed to see them, said, 'I shall not be contented with capturing less than twenty.' He signalled: 'Prepare for battle. Bear up in succession on the course set by the Admiral.'

The approach to battle was a long-drawn ordeal. With all sail set in a feeble breeze and a heavy swell astern, the ships bore down on the enemy at less than a walking pace. The scene became almost festive. Ships that had bands put them up on their poops, where they could plainly be heard by the ships that had none. They all played different tunes, not very well. Boats rowed from ship to ship, and captains hailed each other and wished each other an enemy prize in tow before the night.

NELSON

On the deck of the *Victory*, Nelson was surrounded by friends, and all of them were worried about him. His novel plan put the leading ships of each column in special danger: for the last half mile or so, perhaps for twenty minutes, the *Victory* and Collingwood's *Royal Sovereign* would come under fire from many enemy ships before they could bring their own broadsides to bear. At close quarters, the *Victory* would be the most conspicuous target, and Nelson the most conspicuous figure on her decks. They tried to persuade him to shift his flag to a frigate, or to let another ship lead, or even to cover the stars and decorations on his coat. But avoiding personal danger was not his idea of duty, and he would not listen.

He went down to his cabin during the morning, and wrote a strange codicil to his will, bequeathing Emma and Horatia to the care of the country. Then he knelt at his desk and wrote the prayer that the navy still uses:

May the great God, whom I worship, grant to my country, and for the benefit of Europe in general, a great and glorious victory; and may no misconduct in anyone tarnish it; and may humanity after victory be the predominant feature in the British fleet. For myself individually, I commit my life to him who made me, and may his blessing light upon my endeavours for serving my country faithfully. To him I resign myself and the just cause which is entrusted to me to defend. Amen. Amen. Amen.

That done, he came on deck again in the best of spirits, as he always was in danger. To Blackwood the frigate captain, now one of his closest friends, he said: 'I will now amuse the fleet with a signal. Do you not think there is one yet wanting?'

Blackwood said everyone seemed to know exactly what to do.

'Suppose we telegraph "Nelson confides that every man will do his duty"?'

Someone suggested 'England' instead of 'Nelson', because it would be easier to signal.

'Very well, England,' Nelson said, and he called with an air of boyish gaiety to the signal officer: 'Mr Pasco, I wish to say to the fleet, "England confides that every man will do his duty." You must be quick, for I have one more to make.'

Pasco said 'expects' would be quicker than 'confides'.

'That will do, Pasco, make it directly.'

So the most famous battle signal ever made was hoisted to the yards and mastheads. England expects: it inspired generations of Englishmen. Yet it was not received with unanimous joy in the fleet. Sailors were heard to say 'Do my duty? I've always done my duty, haven't you, Jack?' Nelson's first instinct had been right: it always was in that sort of thing. Nelson confides:

they would have cheered that all right. England was far away; 'expects' seemed mandatory; England was not the navy, and this was a naval occasion. But Nelson was there, one of them, personifying the navy: his confidence was what inspired them. When the flags were hauled down, his last signal was hoisted: 'Engage the enemy more closely.' It flew at the masthead until it was shot away.

At a thousand yards, the *Royal Sovereign* and then the *Victory* came under fire each from the broadsides of half a dozen enemy ships. Against good gunners, Nelson's plan would have been impossible: the leading ships would have been crippled before they could reply. But the French and Spanish after those years in harbour were not good gunners, as Nelson certainly knew; and their ships that morning, with the swell abeam, were rolling heavily, which made them even worse. The *Sovereign* reached the enemy line and disappeared in a cloud of gunsmoke. The *Victory* suffered: the mizzen topmast fell, the wheel was smashed, twenty men were killed before she could fire a shot.

Very slowly, she ploughed on to pistol-shot, and cut through the line astern of the French flagship *Bucentaure*, so close that their rigging touched. She fired her port carronade loaded with a sixty-eight pound ball and a keg of 500 musket balls, and then the awful blast of the whole of her port broadside point blank at the unprotected stern of the *Bucentaure*, and the dust of shattered woodwork drifted across her decks. Then on the starboard side she crashed aboard the French *Redoutable*, and the two ships were grappled together.

The dying Nelson, with his physicians and officers in the cockpit of the Victory; *engraving after the painting by Devis*

NELSON

When close action was joined, there was not much more for an admiral to do, and for half an hour in the centre of the fight Nelson walked up and down the quarter deck with Captain Hardy, of the *Victory*. It was habit and custom, and therefore duty, and nothing would have made them change their pace. But up above, sixty feet away in the Frenchman's mizzen top, were musketeers, and one took aim and fired. The ball struck Nelson on the shoulder. 'They've done for me at last,' he said to Hardy.

They carried him down deck after deck to the orlop where the surgeons were busy. Here by the light of a candle lantern occurred the most familiar death-bed scene in English history, the most public of private agonies. The few men who were there met afterwards and wrote down every word he whispered, about Emma and Horatia, and duty and the battle, and the pain. And those words 'Kiss me, Hardy'. Some people ever since have thought them embarrassing, but they were perfectly in character: the man of infinite friendship, entering now the awful solitude of dying and needing the last touch of human warmth. We know the scene so well that it seems unreal, like a play; but to each man who knew what was happening it had a terrible tragic reality, because each of them felt a friend was dying there. It lasted two hours before an unknown hand wrote in pencil in the *Victory's* log:

4.30. A victory having been reported to the Right Honourable Lord Viscount Nelson, K.B. and Commander-in-chief, he died of his wound.

It was a victory so total, so complete, that sea warfare practically ceased for a century. Yet, as darkness fell that night, men saw that the lantern the *Victory* carried as flagship was extinguished; and their pride in the battle they had won was extinguished too, in sorrow for this man they had lost. 'My heart is rent with the most poignant grief:' so Collingwood wrote, in the official dispatch that should have been written in triumph. Captain Blackwood wrote to his wife: 'On such terms, it was a victory I never wished to have witnessed.' Hardy wrote: 'His death I shall for ever mourn.' A sailor: 'Our dear Admiral Nelson is killed. Chaps that fought like the devil sit down and cry like a wench.' And Dr Scott, who was Nelson's secretary: 'When I think, setting aside his heroism, what an affectionate fascinating little fellow he was, I become stupid with grief.'

These men were not sentimentalists, except perhaps Dr Scott: they were as tough as leather. Yet any sailor even now who reads their letters feels an echo of the same emotion. The fact is that Nelson set the navy a daunting standard of duty, and of compassion; and in good times and bad, in strength and weakness, the navy has not forgotten it. Ever since, when ships have been in danger, men have asked themselves what Nelson would have done; and then they have gone and done it, or died in trying.

THOS. COOK & SON

JOHN PUDNEY

Thomas Cook was born thirteen years before railroads and died eleven years before aeroplanes. His business was travel but he saw it as more than mere business. 'God's earth, with all its fullness and beauty, is for the people; and railroads and steamboats are the results of the common light of science, and are for the people also.'

He was a boy when the Duke of Wellington, speaking of railways, saw 'no reason to suppose that these machines will ever force themselves into general use'. He was a young man when the Iron Duke deplored the growth of the new railways on the grounds that they 'would encourage the lower classes to move about'. This is just what Thomas Cook did. Deviously and gradually he encouraged the working people in nineteenth-century industrial Britain to become mobile. He and his son went on to set the middle classes travelling abroad. His business, idealistically, even piously conceived, became a commercial empire. Though he lived to make travel arrangements for his sovereign Queen Victoria, and to carry his name to the ends of the earth, nothing could have been more basically working-class than the origins of Thomas Cook, born in the heart of pre-industrial England at Melbourne, Derbyshire, in 1808.

His birthplace, No. 9 Quick Close, a semi-detached worker's cottage, was adorned with a commemoration bronze in the 1950s inscribed *He made world travel easier*. It has been swept away, and the area is now part of the self-assertive, industrialised Midland scene in which the name Thomas Cook is most likely to conjure up this year's or next year's package tour. When Thomas first saw light there, in the reign of George III, Melbourne was deep set in the traditional rustic landscape which still belonged to the eighteenth century: landlocked, far from the sea, from capital cities. It was a world in which country people never and townsfolk seldom moved about, except from necessity – and then by wagon or barge, but mostly on foot. Only the very privileged travelled for pleasure.

The insularity of Thomas Cook's birth, upbringing and early life contrast strangely with his global achievement. He started work at ten. At twenty he had never seen a railway or talked with any individual who had been abroad. He himself was nearly fifty before he set foot outside the British Isles. He never spoke any language but English – with the unadorned accent of the Leicester men of his time.

The Cooks were a family of strict Baptists, their lives shaped by nonconformity, respectability, hardship and hard work. The father, occupation unknown, died when Thomas was three. His mother married again, and had more children. She and the step-father James Smithard did their best for the boy. He could at least read and write when he was taken away from school to augment the family income. How slender those resources were is suggested by his earnings of sixpence a week from one of the local market gardeners, John Roby.

When Thomas was about fourteen years old, in 1822, it was decided that he should be indentured to his uncle, John Pegg, a wood-turner and cabinet-maker. As a reward for steady application, he gradually acquired a skill, not only with the lathe but in other aspects of the turner's and cabinet-maker's craft. Yet his new work was often tedious. He learnt the drudgery of ripping ash planks with a handsaw into the pieces from which farm-tool shafts were turned. To get through his stint and later have some time for fishing in the Trent, his favourite pleasure, he would often begin work at two or three in the morning, keeping himself going on a little milk saved from overnight. These industrious habits must have been native; they seem to have owed little to the example of his master. 'The turner sought his relaxation and enjoyment night after night,' to quote a possibly biased account from *The Temperance Mirror* of 1889, 'in a snug corner in the village public-house, where much of his time was wasted and his means so dissipated that, notwithstanding a good business, he lived and died a poor man.'

Young Thomas had entered the fellowship of the Baptish Church. He had also started climbing in through the windows of Melbourne chapel to practise preaching. But religious fervour was not the sole source of his drive, his inspired sense of mission which would, almost quixotically, develop into a dream world of travel. The catalyst for him was Drink.

During the eighteenth century, legislation had encouraged the distillation of spirits in England to counter the importation of foreign brandy. The consumption of cheap gin, particularly among the workers in the cities, was enormous. Bad social conditions, of course, had as much to do with it as appetite. 'Drunk for a penny, dead drunk for twopence, clean straw for nothing' was the dram-shops' invitation to those in search of solace or oblivion. The situation was hardly different when the government under Wellington, in its collective wisdom, decided that more beer would mean less spirits; and the Beerhouse Act of 1830 was passed. This provided 'that any householder desirous of selling malt liquor, by retail, in any house, may obtain an excise licence on payment of two guineas, and for cider only, on paying one guinea'. Beerhouses might be open from 4 a.m. until 10 p.m., except during the hours of divine service on Sundays and holy days.

Thirty thousand new beerhouses were opened at once, and within six years of the passing of the Act this number had increased to more than 44,000. Certainly, as the Act intended, more beer was drunk. But so, too, was more spirit. For the distillers met the competition of the beerhouses by building more flash gin-palaces, whose glitter attracted custom to such purpose that the consumption of British-distilled spirits increased by a third during the decade of 1830-39. Sydney Smith reported: 'The new Beer Bill has begun its operations. Everybody is drunk. Those who are not singing are sprawling. The sovereign people are beastly drunk.'

Though Thomas Cook kept his basic livelihood as a wood-turner, his whole nature was bound up in Baptist missionary work and the promotion of Temperance. How lovingly he came to know that green heart of England – the modest geography of his first travels. He was already keeping a diary and in 1829 he recorded that he travelled 2692 miles – 2106 on foot. He was twenty, he was in love, and he was working contentedly within a small compass set in the centre of England. The world outside, the ways of life being revolutionised by steam power, the new railways, steamships, the world of mobility in which he was to be one of the prime movers, was remote indeed.

He had taken the pledge: 'I agree to abstain from ardent spirits, and to discountenance the causes and practice of intemperance.' Not as yet teetotal; that came later. Meanwhile he married a farmer's daughter at Barrowden and looked forward to family life based on wood-turning, preaching and promoting Temperance. Little did he realise how his ideals were about to converge with the new materialism which was locomotion. The good cause and the new railroads were indeed destined to go it together.

What were the new railways doing socially as they began to network the country commercially? Charles Greville wrote from Knowsley on a July day in 1837 when the railways were not yet ten years old:

Tired of doing nothing in London I resolved to vary the scene and run down here to see the Birmingham railroad, Liverpool, and Liverpool races. So I started at five o'clock on Sunday evening, got to Birmingham at half-past five on Monday morning, and got upon the railroad at half-past seven. Nothing can be more comfortable than the vehicle in which I was put, a sort of chariot with two places, and there is nothing disagreeable about it but the occasional whiffs of stinking air which it is impossible to exclude altogether. The first sensation is a slight degree of nervousness and a feeling of being run away with, but a sense of security soon supervenes, and the velocity is delightful . . . There were all sorts of people going to Liverpool races, barristers to the assizes, and candidates to their several elections.

Five years later Queen Victoria made her first journey by rail, and from Buckingham Palace wrote to her uncle, the King of the Belgians: 'We arrived here yesterday morning, having come by the railroad from Windsor, in half an hour, free from dust and crowd and heat, and I am quite charmed with it.'

So the new railways were acceptable to the great and good, the leisured and the monied, and from the beginning a class system prevailed. For a common man and his wife, the working classes, if they *had* to travel there were open trucks in which they stood up to enjoy the rare privilege of going about.

Excursions for pleasure had been made before Thomas Cook had his first inspiration. Two Mechanics' Institutes had exchanged visits at reduced fares. Special trains had run on the Whitby and Pickering line in aid of the Church Building fund. A really sinister pleasure trip had run in 1838 to Bodmin to witness a public execution. The gallows were in full sight of the uncovered station, so it was not even necessary for the passengers to leave the open railway carriages.

It was 1841, the year before Queen Victoria herself took to the railway, that Thomas Cook felt himself stirred by what was happening very locally. His great moment of inspiration came to him at the age of thirty-three. There was no story that he liked to tell more in after years. He was travelling, as was his wont, on foot:

About midway between Harborough and Leicester – my mind's eye has often reverted to the spot – a thought flashed through my brain – what a glorious thing it would be if the newly-developed powers of railways and locomotion could be made subservient to the promotion of temperance! That thought grew upon me as I travelled over the last six or eight miles. I carried it up to the platform, and strong in the confidence of sympathy of the Chairman, I broached the idea of engaging a special train to carry the friends of temperance from Leicester to Loughborough and back, to attend a quarterly delegate meeting appointed to be held there in two or three weeks following. The Chairman approved, the meeting roared with excitement . . .

He put up his scheme to the secretary of the Midland Counties Railway Company and got a straight answer. 'I know nothing of you or your Society but you shall have the train.'

Though the train was the largest item in this great adventure – twenty to twenty-five open carriages called 'tubs' – the filling of them was a considerable pioneering task. For the first time young Cook was really organising and marshalling people. That cherished word *arrangements*, which was never to leave his lips for long, made its debut.

At Loughborough, arrangements for a gala and for feeding the multitude. Arrangements with the public-spirited Mr Paget for the use of his Park for the multitude. Arrangements for gathering in the multitude from Nottingham, Derby and other places. Arrangements for bands and banners, for the printing of posters and tickets for the multitude who were to travel from Leicester to Loughborough and back. Eleven miles each way, for a shilling.

5 July 1841 was the great day which founded the fortunes of Thos. Cook, though he little knew it at the time.

The number who availed themselves of this train, [wrote the *Leicester Chronicle* reporter], was exactly 485; and, as many came at a later hour by the regular train, there could not be fewer than 500 Leicester folk present at the festival. These intrepid teetotallers were packed standing in the seatless tubs. Few of them had been aboard a train before. Many had never travelled so far as eleven miles in any conveyance. They stood as all third class passengers had to – exposed to the elements and to the soot and sparks given off by the engine, and dazzled by the novelty of smooth speed. They went accompanied by an excellent band, and were headed by their district officers and flags. When they arrived at Loughborough, they were met by the Teetotallers of that town, and the two parties walked in procession from the station into the town, to Mr Paget's park . . .

After tea, dancing, cricket, kiss-in-the-ring and tag, the multitude, some 3000 strong, listened to speeches, including of course one by Thos. Cook, which lasted three solid hours.

Then there was the business of getting home. By the time Cook's excursion train returned to Leicester it was nearly dark, but there was still a great crowd to welcome home the pioneers. It was in fact a big splash in a small pond. It was a very localised event. It never occurred to anyone, least of all to Thomas Cook, that the business of travel or the running of excursions could become a full-time occupation. Even in his mid-thirties he still saw himself as a preacher and missionary, baptismally active, as an 1844 report suggests:

Cook's first excursion train en route from Leicester to Loughborough, July 1841; from a later drawing

At Smeeton, near Leicester, three persons were baptised in the Canal. The baptism was to have taken place in a small rivulet, which had been prepared for the purpose, but during the previous night, some mischievous persons broke down the embankment. This, however, resulted in the furtherance, rather than the hindrance, of the cause of truth, as a more suitable place was found. From 800 to 1000 spectators were present, who listened with marked attention of an address by Mr T. Cook, Leicester, who afterwards immersed the candidates.

By this time he had become quite a hand at excursionism. A notable feat of piety and enterprise had been the snatching of Sunday School children out of temptation's way during Leicester Races.

On the first day, he recalled, 3000 children were conveyed in every kind of vehicle that could be mustered, including a number of new, never-before-used iron coal wagons. The ordinary rolling-stock was inadequate to the occasion; and, with the wagon supplements filled to their utmost capacity, we still left behind 1500 little enthusiasts for a second day!

A feature of that excursion was the self-assured appearance of a ten-year-old boy with a white teetotaller's wand in his hand. 'With this, according to an eye-witness, 'he gravely indicated to his fellow passengers – most of whom were neither older nor bigger than himself – where they were to go, while he also told them what they were to do.'

This, on his first public duty, was John Mason Cook, destined to world renown as the 'and Son' of the firm's title. The first fame of this only son was localised but significant. At a time when hard liquor was taken for granted as essential nourishment for infants, the boy had been brought up teetotal, and was thus a veritable symbol of temperance. He had been taken on the first excursion and had participated in all the father's activities, religious and secular. The father-son partnership – *The Times* in the nineties called them 'the Julius and Augustus of modern travel' – presented a façade of public inseparability as solid and benign as any commercial landmark in Victorian England. They were indeed complementary. Both were opportunists, Father Cook the initiator, the imaginative idealist; and Cook the son the consolidator, who accepted idealism but put business first.

In the 1840s Thomas Cook abandoned wood-turning for printing and publishing, and as soon as the son was old enough he dutifully joined his father's new trade. Established at Leicester, Cook edited, published and printed works such as *The Temperance Messenger, The Children's Temperance Magazine*, and *The Anti-Smoker and Progressive Temperance Reformer*. His zeal for temperance was undiminished, but other notions came rushing in. 'We rejoice to be of the number who are opposed to *all war*. I am a man of peace and a member of the Peace Society,' he declared.

He was also opposed to drink, tobacco, and all the sins of the Victorian world but he believed in liberating people. In 1844 he cried: 'We must have railways for the millions.' He saw railways as a social force. He became a great prophet of the principle of the greatest benefit for the greatest number at the lowest cost. 'It is delightful to see, as we travel on, the breaking down of partition walls of prejudice, the subduing of evil passions and unhappy tempers.' Such sentiments tended to fade with the beginning of the hard business of travel. Romantic aspects were never overlooked. 'How often has it been that a young gentleman has taken a through ticket to some distant place, and ere he got halfway through his intended journey some fair charmer has unwittingly drawn him in another direction . . .'

By the 1840s the annual holiday was becoming part of British family life for those who could afford it. But for the lower middle and working classes holiday with travel was a ravishing novelty – a dream which Cook was making it his business to turn into a reality. Nevertheless he called it a fancy – his first excursion to break out of the flat Midlands across water and up mountains. After five years as an 'amateur' part-time excursionist, 'my fancies took a wider and higher flight and I proposed an excursion from Leicester, Nottingham and Derby to Liverpool, where I engaged a special steamer to go to Bangor, and through the Menai Straits to Caernarvon, with a second supplement, by "Shanks' naggie" to the summit of Snowdon.'

The advertisements for this trip created a sensation. At Leicester there was a brisk trade in tickets at double their face value. A second trip was improvised to meet public demand. The dramatic moment for Cook came at 'the top of Snowdon, from which point I looked toward Ben Lomond and Ben Nevis and determined to get to Scotland the next year, or know the reason why'.

Scotland! The magic tartan world of Walter Scott, of Burns, misty landscapes with deer by Landseer – and nobody mentioned the Highland Clearances when well-heeled Waverley-minded tourists flocked across the border. It was enough that the Queen herself with Albert was establishing their romantic holiday home at Balmoral. Here was a dream world indeed.

But he had set himself a formidable task. No railway crossed the border (and none would for another two years) so the excursion was routed from Leicester to Fleetwood, thence to Ardrossan by steamer, and on to Glasgow by rail. He had three hundred and fifty people on his hands. The gentle shepherding of the first excursions gave way to an assured conducting in which nothing was tentative, nothing left to chance. These were mostly wage-earning people who had rarely if ever left home, to

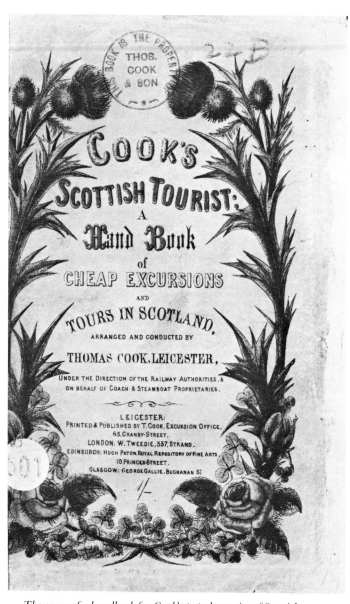

THIS BOOK IS THE PROPERTY

THOS.
COOK
& SON

Cook's
Scottish Tourist:
A
Hand Book
of
CHEAP EXCURSIONS
AND
TOURS IN SCOTLAND,
ARRANGED AND CONDUCTED BY
THOMAS COOK, LEICESTER,
UNDER THE DIRECTION OF THE RAILWAY AUTHORITIES, &
ON BEHALF OF COACH & STEAMBOAT PROPRIETARIES.

LEICESTER:
PRINTED & PUBLISHED BY T. COOK, EXCURSION OFFICE,
65, CRANBY-STREET,
LONDON: W. TWEEDIE, 337, STRAND.
EDINBURGH: HUGH PATON, ROYAL REPOSITORY OF FINE ARTS,
10, PRINCES-STREET.
GLASGOW: GEORGE GALLIE, BUCHANAN ST

1/-

The cover of a handbook for Cook's popular series of Scottish tours,
which lasted from 1846 to 1863

whom leisure travel was a challenging novelty. From the start Cook led them by exhortation. 'Parties will have to be wide awake at an early hour, or they will be disappointed. Promptitude on the part of the Railway Company calls for the same from passengers.'

They got their money's worth. The adventure of a dirty night sea-crossing was followed by a salute of guns as their train pulled into Glasgow; and a band of music to escort them to the City Hall for what were described as 'noble speeches'. Then Edinburgh. Another soirée, more speeches. Stirling by the Forth Steamers, Loch Lomond, and the Burns country – and back to Leicester, replete with travellers' tales.

For the next fifteen years Thomas spent some two months of each summer conducting parties to and through Scotland. These tours were the staple of his business in the earlier days. In 1847, he declared:

I followed the Queen and Prince Albert over the route which they made royal, by the Clyde, the Kyles of Bute, the Crinan Canal, and the Atlantic coast to Oban; from thence to Staffa and Iona, circumnavigating the island of Mull and afterwards visiting Glendor, Fort William and the Caledonian Canal to Inverness. The great Highland coach road between Inverness, Dunkeld and Perth became a favourite route long ere the first sod of a railway was turned.

It could have been the influence of the Queen acting upon a stirring of female emancipation which encouraged ladies to join the Highland tours. From first to last Cook welcomed the fair sex:

Of the thousands of tourists who have travelled with us, the majority have been ladies. In family parties, the preponderance is generally on the feminine side; but there are also great numbers of ladies who start alone, and always meet with agreeable company and get through without any particular inconvenience or discomfort. As to their energy, bravery, and endurance of toil, as a rule they are fully equal to those of the opposite sex, whilst many of them frequently put to shame the 'Masculine' effeminates. The trappings of prevailing fashion may sometimes perplex them in climbing over precipices, and amongst rude blocks of granite and basalt; but there is a large class, who, defiant of fashion or customs . . . push their way through all difficulties, and acquire the perfection of tourist character.

Chambers the Edinburgh publisher had called him a Field Marshal: he had referred to himself as Napoleon. Did the Scottish business with its abundance of admiring, sometimes adoring, female customers turn his head? It inflated his ego, no doubt, but that ego was very much in the service of God, teetotalism and humanity. What makes him larger than life-size, even for those times, was his imaginative versatility.

While the Scottish trips prospered he was broadening his interests in Leicester. Mrs Cook – an efficient and flexible lady by all accounts – had been set up to manage a Temperance Hotel. Though he was a purveyor of pleasure, Thomas was not indifferent to the social unrest sweeping

Leicester Temperance Hall, 1840

through the country. In the mid-1840s, when Peel was abolishing the Corn Laws and saving England from revolution, Cook answered the call of 'cheap bread for the millions'. He published a little paper called *The Cheap Bread Herald*, the main object of which was the downfall of Protection. To this he added personal appearances. 'It was my practice on every Monday and Friday evening to make announcements from my window in Granby Street of the Corn Law Appeal. On such evenings, there generally collected together about a thousand people to list to my statements from the public window of my house . . . ' He also went into soup and potatoes:

I engaged in another practical work for the benefit of the poor. I undertook preparation of soup, upon which I expended for materials £500. I made for distribution through the town 15,000 gallons of very strong superior soup. During the potato famine I bought several boat loads of potatoes in Northamptonshire, brought them to the port of the borough near the river Soar, where they were sold in small quantities at prime cost . . .

Repeal of the Corn Laws and free trade heralded the beginning of years of Victorian prosperity. The Great Exhibition in Hyde Park in 1851 set the tone of achievement for Victoria's subjects, not least for the Cooks.

THE WONDER OF 1851!

FROM YORK

TO LONDON AND BACK FOR A CROWN.

THE MIDLAND RAILWAY COMPANY

Will continue to run

TWO TRAINS DAILY

(Excepted Sunday, when only one Train is available)

FOR THE GREAT EXHIBITION,

UNTIL SATURDAY, OCTOBER 11,

Without any Advance of F

RETURN SPECIAL TRAINS leave the Euston Station on MONDAYS, TUESDAYS, THURSDAYS, & SATURDAYS at 11 a.m., on WEDNESDAYS and FRIDAYS at 1 p.m., and EVERY NIGHT (Sundays excepted) at 9 p.m.

First and Second Class Tickets are available for returning any day (except Sunday) up to and including Monday, Oct. 20. Third Class Tickets issued before the 6th instant are available for 14 days, and all issued after the 6th are returnable any day up to Monday the 20th.

The Trains leave York at 9-40 a.m. every day except Sunday, and also every day, including Sunday, at 7-20 p.m.

Fares to London and Back:--

1st Class 15s. 2nd, 10s, 3rd, 5s.

The Midland is the only Company that runs Trains Daily at these Fares.

Ask for Midland Tickets!

Children above 3 and under 12 years of age, Half-price. Luggage allowed—112 lbs. to First Class, 100 lbs. to Second, and 56 lbs. to Third Class Passengers.

APPROVED LODGINGS, of all classes, are provided in London for Passengers by Midland Trains. The Agents will give Tickets of reference on application, without charge, and an Office is opened in London, at DONALD's WATERLOO DINING ROOMS, 14, Seymour-street, near Euston Station, where an agent is in regular attendance to conduct parties who go up unprepared with Lodgings.

The Managers have much pleasure in stating that the immense numbers who have travelled under their arrangements have been conducted in perfect safety—indeed in the history of the Midland Lines, *no accident, attended with personal injury, has ever happened to an Excursion Train.* In conducting the extraordinary traffic of this Great Occasion the first object is to ensure *safety*, and that object has hitherto been most happily achieved.

With the fullest confidence, inspired by past success, the Conductors have pleasure in urging those who have not yet visited the Exhibition, to avail themselves of the present facilities, and to improve the opportunity which will close on the 11th of October.

All communications respecting the Trains to be addressed to the Managers, for the Company,

John Cuttle & John Calverley, Wakefield;
Thomas Cook, Leicester.

October 2nd, 1851.

T. COOK, PRINTER, 28, GRANBY-STREET, LEICESTER.

Cook's poster advertising his 'Arrangements' for the Great Exhibition of 1851

Thomas Cook, now into his forties, had been constantly letting his thoughts fly off across the Atlantic. But any ambition to discover America was suddenly halted one morning in Derby in 1850 when he met another former gardener's boy, Joseph Paxton, whose last-minute design for what was called 'a blazing arch of lucid glass' had been accepted for the building to house the Great Exhibition. Already there were thousands of men at work in Hyde Park so that the Crystal Palace should be ready for the Queen's opening on May Day 1851. Paxton, in his capacity as a Midland Railway director, persuaded Cook to throw away all thoughts of America in order to run excursions to the Exhibition – and this he did. So overnight he became a railway operator, ably assisted by a very knowledgeable son, who for the time being gave up his own career in the Midlands to work full time on the project.

The elder Cook reveals the competitive business acumen which went with the idealism:

On Monday morning the superintendent of the Midland passenger traffic and myself were up and at it at five o'clock. At that hour we started with a fifteen shilling fare to London and back. At nine o'clock it was down to five shillings from Bradford, Leeds, Sheffield, and other competing points, and at that rate it stood to the close of the Exhibition. It was a time of intense excitement, and all the trains on the line, except the day express, were made available for excursion tickets. Frequently the night mail would be run in from two to six divisions. At the call of the band of music I saw workpeople come out of factories in Bradford, pay five shillings for a ticket, and with a very few shillings in their pockets start off on Saturday night to spend Sunday and Monday in London, returning to work on Tuesday morning. The people of Yorkshire were thus educated to travel, and my returns at the end of the season showed 150,000 who had taken the excursion tickets.

Thomas Cook was a fervent communicator. Tracts and pamphlets poured from him. Until 1854 his business as a general printer and publisher facilitated his own outpourings. At the time of the 1851 Exhibition he established his *Excursionist*, a travel magazine in which he blew his own trumpet very engagingly throughout his lifetime and which continued to appear until the Second World War.

In spite of his London success and his dreams of America he remained resolutely provincial. Though his schemes were beginning to cover the whole country he clung to Leicester. He promoted the Victorian seaside – at the time of his birth nobody thought of lingering on a beach. From the Midlands Everyman and his wife could go, for a matter of shillings, to Scarborough, Morecambe, Blackpool in the north, and Hastings, Brighton, the Isle of Wight in the south.

As the novelty of actually going by train wore off, Cook developed the flair for topical events which he had shown at the time of the Great

*It was Cook above all who made seaside holidays possible for the
sort of public shown in these comic postcards*

Exhibition. Exhibitions, Galas, moonlight trips to the Manchester Exhibition, and a special excursion to see Brunel's famous *Great Britain* Steamship stranded in Dundrum Bay, Ireland, in 1848.

In May 1855 – with the Crimean War going strong – Thomas Cook at last set foot abroad. The Paris Exhibition, opened by the Emperor Napoleon III, had immediate appeal. The French were our allies: and such an Exhibition was symbolic of progress. Cook seized the opportunity but found that not everybody would play.

I tried hard to induce the companies commanding the Channel traffic to give me facilities to work with them and for them. But they could not or would not see it to be to their advantage to comply with my requests, and the only cheap facility I could get was by the Great Eastern route via Harwich to Antwerp . . . This opened the way for a grand circular tour.

The first Cook-conducted tour across the Channel was recorded in the journal of a certain Miss Matilda – and of course published later in the *Excursionist*:

Mr Cook has mapped out for us a most delightful route. We visited Antwerp, Brussels, Cologne, Mayence, Mannheim, Heidelberg, Strasbourg and Paris . . . Many of our friends thought us too independent and adventurous to leave the shores of old England, and thus plunge into foreign countries not beneath Victoria's sway, with no protecting relatives, but we can only say that we hope this will not be our last excursion of this kind. We could venture anywhere with such a guide and guardian as Mr Cook for there was not one of his party but felt perfectly safe when under his care. We calculate an estimate of our expenses for travelling, guides, hotels etc. for ladies, to be about £10.0s.0d. for a fortnight's trip.

Cook wrote significant footnotes. 'One party of half-a-dozen confident travellers broke off from us at Kehl for a tour into and through Switzerland. With considerable difficulty they made their way, and thus started in my mind an idea of Swiss Tours.'

Two more exhibitions cropped up to delight Thomas Cook with the realisation of his dream of moving masses of working class people to entertainments of an improving character. The first, in Paris again, gave him valuable continental experience:

Early in 1861 a proposal had been made by a London committee to get up a cheap working men's demonstration for Paris. Difficulties beset the committee, and I joined hands with them. Sir Joseph Paxton, at my request, accepted the position of President, and exerted his powerful influence on behalf of the project. I undertook to work the country in the Midland and Northern districts, and at Whitsuntide we took over the Channel from 1,500 to 1,600 visitors, more than 800 of whom came up from country stations. The affair went off well, and the presence of Sir Joseph Paxton in Paris gave tone to the arrangements. I tried to repeat the idea at Whitsuntide, 1862, but I was crippled by conditions, the prices were enhanced, and the effort was a comparative failure.

More important was the Exhibition at Brompton in 1862, which in fact drew more people than the 1851 Exhibition in Hyde Park. On this occasion the whole Cook family was to be involved, providing not only the means of getting there but accommodation for the workers from the industrial areas. This was valuable experience in the accommodation of large numbers of people and it also finally convinced Thomas of the need for a base in London.

As nothing at the Exhibition was for sale, Cook set up an International Bazaar and Scotch Court opposite the main entrance. Here were pebble jewellery, tartan souvenirs, Edinburgh rock and shortbread, with lithographs of the Prince Consort, Lord Macaulay and Thomas Cook himself. An Aberdeen outfitter offered The Excursionist Tweed Suit at forty-five shillings. The walls, predictably, were decorated with antlers and deer's heads. And of course the most prominent feature was Cook's office for the issue of Scottish Tourist Tickets.

But much of this was in vain. At the end of 1862 the Scottish railway managers refused to allow him to issue any more tickets, having decided to take the excursion business into their own hands. Cook protested in vain and in print declared: 'Beyond the present season all is in obscurity. Our desire is to follow the leadings of Providence: to live while we live to some useful purpose, cultivating and strengthening those influences which, ripened and matured on earth, bear fruit beyond the grave.' Providence led him to two decisive steps. To focus his tourist ambitions south across the Channel and to set up in London the British Museum Boarding House in Great Russell Street.

Cook's London headquarters were in a small conservatory and there Charles Dickens sent his reporter Edmund Yates to write for his *All the Year Round* an article facetiously called 'My Excursion Agent'.

The front door of this house, on which was a large brass plate duly inscribed with the excursion agent's honoured name, stood open, and by the side of a glass door within, where the visitor's hall is usually to be found, I read the word 'Office', and, entering, found my agent awaiting my anticipated arrival. The house is, as I afterwards learned, a private hotel, but, the neighbours objecting to anything as low as a public announcement on a board, my agent defers to their prejudices, and describes his house as a boarding-house or receptacle for his customers while in town.

For a few years the conservatory made do as an office while Mrs Cook and daughter Annie looked after the transit tourists who put up at the hotel. For Thomas Cook these were to be the exciting years of the

The Britisher abroad: a sketch at Notre Dame, Paris, in 1882

discovery for himself – and for his followers – of foreign parts.

He was over fifty and a grandfather when he made his first journey to negotiate with the French railways. In Paris he made contracts both with transport people and with hotel proprietors. Nothing was left to chance. The money side of it was keenly argued and firmly arranged. These agreements with the French formed the foundation of the essentially international character of his empire.

Though it was not too late in life to girdle the globe, it was too late to study grammar. How did he manage without a word of any foreign language? Dickens's man wondered about that:

I suggested that his knowledge of foreign languages must be severely taxed. Then he smiled, and told me that was provided for by his knowing nothing but English; but that mattered little, as there was always one of his party at his elbow to explain what he suggested.

Cook was playing up to the Press there. He couldn't have left such a vital matter to chance, while he made sure his tourists went unscathed, unrobbed and stimulated within limits.

He might pay heavy attention to moral values, but he maintained his championship of the rights of ladies to travel alone – with his protection and advice. 'Ladies may, without impropriety, visit the best cafés, or sit at the tables outside. Ladies should, however, on no account enter the cafés on the north side of the Boulevards, between the Grand Opera and the Rue St Denis.'

People of modest means, described by Dickens's reporter as 'tradesmen and their wives, merchants, clerks away for a week's holiday, smart mechanics', made up the first 578 excursionists, who in 1862 went to Paris on probably the first ever package tour. They were conducted personally by Cook, and had benefited from the following advice:

We would have every class of British subjects visit Paris, that they may emulate its excellencies, and shun the vices and errors which detract from the glory of the French capital. In matters of taste and courtesy, we may learn much from Parisians; and on some questions of morality we may have right views strengthened. We would have a sober and steady Englishman go to Paris to learn how to value his Christian privileges, especially those relating to the Lord's Day . . . Give us a quiet Highland Sabbath . . . in preference to the triviality, mirth and labour of a continental Sunday.

In spite of such moralising he was on the threshold of creating *le playground de l'Europe* in Switzerland. Indeed the official record credits him jointly with the British Alpine Club with founding Swiss Tourism. This was good business, good Victorian enterprise. But what made him do it? What drove him on? It was surely the imagination of a romantic, who talked in platitudes of the 'land of Tell', who had looked from the summit of Snowdon to the mountains of Scotland, and from Ben Lomond towards the Alps. And from Chamonix on first arrival in June 1863 he declared: 'Can it be possible that I am sitting at the foot of the Monarch of the Alps? . . . But how came I here? What object brought me here? And what am I doing here?' He soon got down to brass tacks. 'The fares to Switzerland will be the cheapest ever advertised, and the whole journey may be accomplished for the amount of a moderate Scotch trip.'

Toward the end of that first Swiss trip with sixty-two excursionists, many of them ladies, Thomas Cook was fairly carried away:

These hills and peaks were being covered with a twilight veil, when suddenly was seen a full and glorious moon ascending majestically over those white Jura peaks, and casting rays of light and glory over the still waters. Just at that moment a band of music struck up sweet notes on the Neuchâtel shore, and several boating parties of ladies and gentleman chanted evening songs of thrilling melody. The scene and sounds were those in which fairies are represented as revelling in their unearthly ecstasies; and truly it was a scene to make the weary mountain climbers forget their weariness, and breathe the sweetest air of evening repose.

This first trip proved that the Swiss readily took to the idea of organised

Determined ladies tackle the Alps, c.1875

excursionists and that Switzerland could be for everyone – or nearly everyone. No longer just for the nobility on the grand tour, the landed gentry, the opulent who had rather superciliously 'done' Europe after the Napoleonic Wars. Nevertheless Cook was beginning to cater less for the humble wage-earner and more for the new bourgeoisie and professional classes thrown up by industrial prosperity at home and trade and exploitation overseas.

For Thomas it was romance, business acumen, and missionary zeal all hand in hand. For his filial partner, from now on it was business acumen first and last, served by fantastic energy, expert knowledge, a commanding presence, and a highly developed imaginative flair. He had been persuaded to abandon his own printing business in Leicester to become full-time partner to manage the first London office established in Fleet Street and to assist his father in pioneering Europe. In the winter of 1865 they made an exploratory trip to Switzerland and Italy. How well they were established in Paris is reflected in the younger man's notes:

On arriving in Paris we met with the usual hearty reception, and received the usual kindnesses from everyone with whom we had to transact in business, and it was exceedingly gratifying to find the Directors and Managers of Railways and Diligences were also perfectly satisfied with the result of last season's labour, that several opportunities were offered of extending our tourist arrangements.

Father and son went on to cross the St Gotthard Pass in sleighs:

The snow continued falling, and as we neared the summit the wind arose, and in addition to the falling snow drifted considerable quantities off the mountain, but through the whole ascent the writer never felt any painful sensation of cold . . . and going into the Hospice at the summit, he suffered from hot-ache which soon passed off, and after having a café noir (without the cognac) was quite ready for the descent to Airolo.

In his first year Cook sent six hundred tourists to Switzerland. In the third year Thos. Cook and Son – henceforth that was the name – sent nearly two thousand. And it went on from there – until there were young ladies swarming over the mountains and, like Jemima Morrell, writing their journals:

Waking at four o'clock there was a rustle in the household; at four thirty the Travellers break-fasted, and at six some 130 tourists who were travelling under Mr Cook's guidance, and his Tickets, started from London Bridge Station for Newhaven . . .

In Switzerland Miss Jemima paid close attention to the food. Her lunch at Geneva consisted of ten courses, including soup, salmon, roast beef, boiled fowl, sweetbreads, roast fowl, artichokes and several kinds of dessert. It seems to have met with everyone's approval, but the same could not be said for the service, which Miss Jemima criticised several times throughout the journey for being too nimble. She complained that each dish would be placed for a moment on a silver stand, whereupon,

being, it is supposed, duly eyed by the company, it is removed to be carved by an official aside, whose dexterity in dissection is only surpassed by the agility of the waiter who, if for a second you lay down your knife and fork, makes a dart at your plate like a cobra's and carries off your *bonne bouche* as his prey.

The Miss Jemimas – and there were many of them – might smile at strange foreign customs, criticise the service and stay aloof from actually meeting the natives but they relied on Cook, as a father-figure – a father-figure hired at a prearranged price – to see them through the experience. And as a father-figure he saw himself more and more as time went on. In 1864 he was already calling his customers 'Cook's people'. 'There is an identity in the successive character of our visits and visitors, and we hope to see "Cook's people" as distinctly recognised in their social travelling arrangements in Switzerland as they have been in Scotland and elsewhere.'

Charles Dickens's reporter questioned him about the customers:

The destination of the excursion, he explained, greatly determined its numbers and the social classes from which it was made up. The trips to Edinburgh, and the excursions in England, attract tradesmen and their wives, merchants' clerks away for a week's holiday, roughing it with a knapsack, and getting over an immense number of miles before they return; swart mechanics, who seem never to be able entirely to free themselves from traces of their life-long labour, but who are by no means the worst informed, and are generally the most interested about the places they visit.

As to Swiss excursions, the company is of a very different order; the Whitsuntide trip has a good deal of the Cockney element in it, and is mostly composed of very high-spirited people, whose greatest delight in life is 'having a fling', and who do Paris, and rush through France, and through Switzerland to Chamouny (sic), compare every place they are taken to with the views which formed part of the exhibition at the Egyptian Hall, carry London everywhere about with them in dress, habits, and conversation, and rush back, convinced that they are great travellers. From these roysterers the July and September excursionists differ greatly; ushers and governesses, practical people from the provinces, and representatives of the better style of the London mercantile community, who form their component parts, all travel as if impressed with the notion that they are engaged in fulfilling the wishes of a lifetime, in a pleasant duty never to be repeated. They stop at all the principal towns, visiting all the curiosities to be seen in them, and are full of discussion among themselves, proving that they are nearly all thoroughly well-up in the subject. Many of them carry books of reference with them, and nearly all take notes.

After Cook's exploratory trip across the Alps with his son, Italy offered immediate territorial expansion:

The dream of months and the hope of years is a realised fact. We have crossed and re-crossed the Alps and have, at the head of a party of fifty enterprising and confiding ladies and gentlemen, penetrated to the very heart of the kingdom of Italy, exploring royal and ducal palaces, revelling with perfect freedom amongst the multifarious and brilliant productions of sculptors, painters, and Italian artists of every name and degree.

The sturdy Midland missionary lived on in the daring excursionist:

In the social aspects of society, Milan and Turin contrast strangely with such places as Bologna and Florence, where we witnessed exhibitions of priestly domination and superstitious abjection of the most distressing character, and we felt as though we could but weep over the abominations and blasphemies of their rites and ceremonies. Never, never can Italy be really free till the light of Truth and Christian simplicity prevails over such solemn fooleries as it was our lot to witness in the streets and squares of Florence, where bloody crucifixes were paraded about by rude boys, and thousands fell on their knees before ridiculous figures and effigies of Virgin and child.

In spite of the hazards of High Popery and the High Alps, 1865 was a triumphant season. After the long-promised discovery of America, in which Thomas Cook travelled ten thousand miles through Canada and the United States in two winter months, the joyous assault on Central and Southern Europe was resumed. The following March Thomas conducted a party across the Alps by sleigh; and by railway and diligence – some of the time with a military escort – through Turin, Florence to Naples, and of course Pompeii. The high spot was Holy week in Rome. Alas, when he reached Florence, Cook learned by letter that there was no accommodation for his flock of fifty in Rome. The Torlonia Palace was offered at £500 for ten days. Cook let his flock have its say – a wise precaution:

This proposal to meet our requirements was at first startling, but on taking it into consideration it was thought by the party that it might be done. As we did not want to be in Rome more than eight days, we resolved first to offer, by telegraph, the sum of £400 for that length of time. The telegraph was employed to carry our proposal, and quickly the reply came that the Palace could only be had for ten days – for the full amount of £500. This reply was submitted to a special meeting of the party at Florence, and we were then authorised, on condition that each of the party paid an extra £4, to close the agreement and secure the Palace.

The story of the tourists in the Palace redounded to the credit of Thos. Cook at the time and for ever afterwards. He made a slight loss on the transaction, however, and there were ungrateful complaints from tourists to which he replied forthrightly:

We can appreciate the disadvantages under which a great portion of the Palace had to be furnished and provided with the necessary staff for a special occasion, and we have no sympathy with individual expressions of discontent, by which it was attempted to destroy the harmony of the party. Those who travel in Italy must expect sometimes to have to sit on hard seats and place their feet on hard floors, and they will do well if they never fare worse than was our lot in Rome.

As the numbers built up that year the so-called select parties were not always socially amenable and the Father Figure did not hesitate to give them a piece of his mind.

. . . any who cannot accompany us in a genial, sociable and confiding spirit, will be kind enough not to trouble us with their communications or attempt to join our parties. It has been our lot, through many years, to enjoy the greatest social pleasures in these great and responsible undertakings; we have had the confidence and esteem of thousands; our travelling companions have become, in many instances, attached friends; the social feeling has risen above the commercial; and as we began, we desire to continue, and to close this peculiar work, free from petty jarrings and paltry ebullitions of temper or distrust. Those who wish next to accompany us to Italy or elsewhere, will please to note these observations.

The Excursionist took on a more portentous tone:

Bursting the bonds of insularity which have hitherto confined him to the shores of his native island, the Englishman is becoming a travelled man. Every year he and his comrades swarm – in ever increasing numbers – across the Channel . . . Riding, or walking, or sailing, on railway, on high road, or river, Mr Cook's Excursionists pour themselves, like a human flood.

This was too much for Her Majesty's vice Consul at Spezia, Charles James Lever, who had a slight reputation as a novelist and doubled his consular duties with writing pieces for *Blackwood's Magazine* under the pen name Cornelius O'Dowd. 'It seems', he wrote, 'that some enterprising and unscrupulous man has devised the project of conducting some forty or fifty persons, irrespective of age or sex, from London to Naples and back for a fixed sum. He contracts to carry them, feed them, lodge them, and amuse them.'

The Irish wag went on to mention 'a fussy little bald man' – though no names were mentioned – who did the shepherding:

I have already met three flocks and anything so uncouth I never saw before – the men mostly elderly, dreary, sad-looking, evidently bored and tired, the women somewhat younger, travel tossed, and crumpled, but intensely lively, wide awake and facetious. The cities of Italy are deluged with droves of these creatures, for they never separate, and you see them, forty in number, pouring along a street

A picnic on Mount Vesuvius, 1880

with their director – now in the front – now in the rear – circling around them like a sheep dog, and really the process is as like herding as may be.

Thomas Cook treated him in the way he had treated hecklers in the old days in Leicester:

Let me ask why Mr Lever's susceptibilities should be outraged, and his refinement trampled on, because thirty or forty Englishmen and Englishwomen find it convenient to travel in the same train? . . . Reference to a modern compilation shows that this hyper-critical gentleman started upon a career as student of medicine in Dublin, that he subsequently took a German degree, and that after practising for a short time he foresook his profession for novel-writing as being more profitable and less laborious. Apart, then, from his talent for producing fiction – of which I would speak with all possible respect – Mr Lever is an Irish gentleman of the precise class to which the English clergymen, physicians, bankers, civil engineers and merchants, who honoured me by accepting my escort to Italy, indisputably belong. By what right, then, does he constitute himself their censor?

Undoubtedly there was some truth in O'Dowd's assertions, cruel though they were, that

their people, from the hour they set out, regard all foreign countries and their inhabitants as something in which they have a vested right. They have paid for the Continent . . . Europe, in their eyes, is a great spectacle, like a show-piece at Covent Garden; and it is theirs to criticise the performance and laugh at the performers at will.

O'Dowd's private notes to his editor John Blackwood however suggest that he was rather more amused than outraged:

Send for No. 1 of *The Excursionist* edited by a Mr Cook, and if you don't laugh, you're no' the man I thought ye. He pitches into me most furiously for my O'Dowd on the 'Convict Tourists'; and seeing the tone of his paper, I only wonder he did not make the case actionable. He evidently believes that I saw him and takes the whole in the most serious light.

The row did Cook no great harm. Though later *Punch* and a few other journals made a habit of poking fun at excursionists and Cookites, at the time the Press tended to side with him. He also had his active champions. The great George Augustus Sala declared:

Is it not time that the stupid and unjust practice of sneering at Cook's tourists came to an end? . . . I have met with many hundreds of Cook's tourists in the course of my travels; and I never could discern any difference between them and the other English travellers on the Continent, save that they were, as a rule, better behaved and more anxious to acquire information than are the general run of travelling gents of the 'stuck-up' order.

As Thomas's fame spread there was considerable curiosity about him and one witness who confessed herself surprised was a certain Lady Wake, who observed

a quiet, middle-aged man very much like a homestaying, retired tradesman, walking up and down the station with his hands in his pocket, seemingly taking notice of no one. He could not speak a word of any language but his own. How then did he accomplish all these wonders? He had agents in every town, and one line from him could always settle every difficulty and arrange every convenience.

It was his talent as a public relations man that brought Lady Wake within his ambit. She was the sister of the Archbishop of Canterbury, Archibald Campbell Tait, who was in poor health and had been ordered to winter on the Riviera. The Franco-Prussian war then raging prevented direct access from the Channel to the Mediterranean. On hearing of the Archbishop's projected journey, Cook volunteered himself to act as personal courier. The party, including a chaplain, a doctor, servants and children, numbered sixteen.

From the first start we always found most comfortable saloon carriages ready for us, wrote Lady Wake. As we neared each halting place for the night, the landlord of our hotel met us a station in advance, and when we arrived three carriages beautifully appointed were in readiness to convey our party to the hotel, where we found our rooms not only prepared for us but the names of each of our party over the doors, including those of the ladies maids. Cook knew by instinct exactly what would suit each of us.

The trip with the ailing Archbishop was an imaginative piece of opportunism. As the declaration of war had come so suddenly both father and son had to deal with British and American tourists stranded in Europe, some visiting the passion play at Oberammergau. But the conflict was sufficiently localised for them to bring everybody back by circuitous routes. When the Armistice came it was the turn of John Mason Cook to volunteer his services to the Mansion House Committee for the relief of besieged Paris.

He crossed the Channel with members of the Committee and seventy-five tons of provisions from the City of London for the City of Paris. From Dieppe he posted, rode and night-walked by moonlight until on the fourth day he reached the City. He was the first back to report to the Lord Mayor and to suggest that the Parisians then needed not so much provisions as money. But significantly by that time he had also arranged to conduct parties of English sightseers to see defeated Paris during the Armistice, and a party 150 strong left a few days after his return.

This was not the first instance of Cookites craving the sights of war. When the younger Cook led the first parties of excursionists across the Atlantic in the mid-sixties one of the attractions of the New World to these Victorians was a visit to the battlefields of the South. At Fort Harrison,

John Mason Cook, c.1880

John Mason himself recorded the thrill of it all:

The wooden huts that had been headquarters for officers were now used as pig-sties, poultry-houses, and goat houses, for the negroes and other workmen and their families, employed in making a cemetery for burying the bones of the killed. Seventy men were employed for that purpose at the time of our visit. We were conducted to a spinney about one mile to the right of the principal earthworks, where the ground was lost and regained several times in a few hours, and in that part we saw skulls, arms, legs etc., and all bleaching in the sun. In some parts we saw large heaps of bones, some of horses, and others the bones of animals slaughtered as food for the armies. I think all of us brought away some mementoes from this point.

It was the younger Cook who finally consolidated two-way arrangements with America. Among these was a visit (1871) of a party of Knights Templar from Pittsburgh, gorgeous in their masonic paraphernalia. All enjoying the prefix Sir Knight, they were met at Cork by John Mason Cook, who took them on a tour of Ireland and Scotland. Thomas Cook greeted them in London, whence they toured Europe. The arrangements were so successful that their leader, Sir Knight Jenkins, offered to join the firm.

Thus Thomas Cook, Son and Jenkins was established in New York with branches elsewhere. But Sir Knight Jenkins proved to be wildly extravagant and unreliable over money. The Cooks were horrified at the 'liberal and costly fashion' in which the New York office was run, and it all ended with John Mason Cook pursuing the once glamorous Knight in the Law Courts. Without Jenkins the American business went on and prospered, though John Mason, writing to his father toward the end of the seventies that 'your address to Americans is the best business promotion I have seen from your pen for several years and has been sent by this mail . . . ' added: 'I wish most sincerely Christopher Columbus had never found that Western shore.'

By this time it was abundantly clear that John Mason Cook was not a subsidiary figure. He was a forceful character in his own right, immensely strong physically, experienced in the business of travel since childhood. A family man with sons of his own who would be going into the business. Thomas the father had initiated that business but John Mason was really better at it than his father. He had the same imaginative approach and somewhat better organising abilities. Moreover his energies were not dissipated by good works. Thomas wrote of him to his mother that 'he does not like my mixing Missions with business; but he cannot deprive me of the pleasure I have had in the combination . . . I shall neither be expelled from the office nor stifled in my spirit's utterance, and I have told him so very plainly.'

A somewhat unsuccessful concession was made by John Mason to his father's temperance principles when he opened the new offices in Ludgate Circus. He made over some of the upper part of the building for a teetotal press club. Yet despite the patronage of T. P. O'Connor, H. W. Nevison and George Bernard Shaw in his red-bearded days, the journalistic fraternity as a whole failed to support the venture. The move to Ludgate Circus had become necessary because the Fleet Street premises had become too cramped and insignificant. The Headquarters were to stand for more than three decades after father and son were both dead, a symbol of stability, and success, responsibility and respectability. It was a family affair. You could always be safe with Cooks – father and son.

Yet, behind the façade of this temple of travel, father and son wrangled and bickered, and for long periods were not even on speaking terms throughout their prosperous years. Recently letters have come to light reflecting the animosity which smouldered within the divided family. It reached a point when John Mason Cook, having failed to bring about a family conference, wrote a memorandum answering various charges. One of these was 'that I took the monies of the firm to build the Ludgate Circus property without my father's consent and that I have not paid any interest on the monies so used'. He had tried to draw his father's attention to the excellent site on which he proposed to build. His father had shown no personal interest but told him to go ahead.

Upon this understanding I commenced . . . My father never took any part in the matter; I kept telling him from time to time certain things that were going on and he apparently took little interest in them, and to my knowledge never set foot upon the ground or premises until he was compelled to do so on his return to London, after we had removed into the new premises in April 1873.

The memorandum went on to proclaim that nobody had been done down. In a separate note to a lawyer he gave his explanation.

I took money out of the business for the time being and *repaid it all*. My father was . . . fully advised of this. Therefore when you tell me that my father told you that I had applied the partnership assets in carrying out some speculation of my own, I am naturally more anxious than ever to have the matter put perfectly right in black and white.

None of this dissension showed at the Ludgate Circus Headquarters, where he ruled with benign authority. Donald White, famous even in his seventies as the uniformed Cooks' man at Victoria Station, remembered him in earlier days:

A very dapper man, thickset, with a small beard. Very punctual in the mornings. And before entering the office he made a point of inspecting the outside to make sure that posters were clean.

For Victorians in their thousands, the Ludgate Circus headquarters became the threshold of dreams which the Cooks were able to realise for them in comfort and safety. The Holy Land and Egypt, land of the Pharaohs! The Middle East, spice-scented, romantic, and yet a highway of Victorian Empire.

It was above all the Bible that drew Thomas Cook. The paths to the holy places were well trodden. There was a long history of travel from Crusader times – highly organised and expensive. The redoubtable Thomas had to re-organise it for the sort of people who could just afford a hundred guineas, and weeks rather than months away from home. He had encompassed the British Isles, Western Europe and America by steam – rail and boat. Now he took to the horse, the mule, and the Biblical ass, in terrain menaced by brigands and robbers:

Our cavalcade consists of forty saddle horses, sixty baggage mules, twenty-two donkeys with nearly fifty dragomans, servants and muleteers . . . The pleasantest life in Palestine travel is in tents, furnished with iron bedsteads, wool beds, carpeted floors, and an ample supply of excellent, well-cooked food. 'Tim Tom' is generally sounded to wake us up at 6 am (sometimes sooner); in half an hour the tents are struck; in an hour we get breakfast, and by 8 o'clock all is ready for departure. After from four to five hours' riding we rest for a couple of hours where fresh water can be obtained, and where we take lunch. While thus resting, the mules get in advance, and when we arrive at our appointed camping ground we find our movable hotel ready, and resume occupation of the same sleeping apartment, the same bed and bedding, with the same numbered napkin that we left in the morning.

Piety travelled along with them. One of the many clergymen who took part spoke of them joining in psalms as they rode and of evening worship after dinner, their favourite hymn being

> *'And nightly pitch our moving tent*
> *A day's march nearer home . . . '*

Tourists on a Cook's tour of the Holy Land pose with their dragomans before their 'moving tent' in 1903

Cook's office in Jerusalem

There were hazards and adventures. People fell off their mounts. Thomas Cook – yes, there was a twinkle in his eye – called it 'saluting the ground'. When the party passed through Bedouin territory the dragomans and muleteers fired their rifles, while a travelling trumpeter blew aggressively and sang wild songs. The weather sometimes harassed them. A storm blew down all the tents one night and the party had to sleep it out in mud huts. A lady died at three in the morning on another occasion and had to be secretly packed up and carried into Jerusalem to be buried. But meals were regular, heavy and British.

It was Thomas, too, who initiated the wonderful business of the Nile. Egypt was very much in the news when he set out in 1869. De Lesseps was planning to open his Suez Canal by the end of the year. The Prince and Princess of Wales were having a preview and were also doing the Nile. Thomas with thirty-two ladies and gentlemen of the new travelling middle class followed them in two Nile steamers. He wrote somewhat ecstatically:

We have not been able to overtake our own cherished Prince and his beloved Princess . . . and thus our hopes of giving the heir-apparent of the English throne and his amiable Princess a really English cheer on the Nile were frustrated . . . It would have been a real pleasure to have fallen in with this Royal tourist party.

In the royal retinue was the famous W. H. Russell of *The Times* who had reported the Crimean War and was ready to be outraged at the Cook presence.

Cook's tourists have arrived! Their steamers are just below us in the stream. The tourists are all over the place. Some are bathing off the beaches; others with eccentric head-dresses are toiling through the deep sand after an abortive attempt to reach Philae. They are just beaten by a head in the race. Another day, and the Prince and Princess would have been at their mercy!

No sooner was he back from this adventure than Thomas was promising another excursion in that year for the opening of the Suez Canal, which was to be one of the glamorous events of the century. He had booked the Austrian Lloyd steamer *America*, and announced:

This trip will be dirt cheap, in the face of the monstrous impositions that may be expected in Egypt, where the Khedive has bought up all the chief hotel accommodation at the fabulous rate of £2.8s per day for each guest . . . The *America* will form part of the grand Steamboat Procession through the Canal to the Red Sea.

So Cook and his tourists followed the Empress Eugénie through the canal, and took part in perfect safety in the lavish festivities which the occasion called for. It was Thomas Cook's brainwave to place and keep his party on a steamer. This set the pattern for future operations. The Cooks realised that success in countries such as Egypt depended upon isolating their tourists from the unacceptable realities and extreme poverty, squalor and disease which went with the wealth and glamour of Egypt, the Nile and the antiquities. Prosperous Americans and the industrially-rich culture-thirsty middle classes of Britain provided an inexhaustible supply of customers.

Thomas Cook started it, but it was John Mason Cook who moved into Egypt in a big way. He began by hiring a couple of Nile steamers. By 1870 he had himself officially appointed by the Khedive to act as the agent of his Government for passenger traffic on the Nile. In 1875 he persuaded the Egyptian government to pass a passenger steamer over the first cataract in order that there should be a regular steam-boat service from there to the second cataract. By 1880 the Egyptian government granted the firm exclusive control of all passenger steamers and re-fitting of boats, conducting the service at their own expense and risk. The Cooks ended by owning their own fleet of steamers, with a Nile shipyard.

The secret was that Cook created for his customers a floating dream. A miniature Grand Hotel, but with a very English club atmosphere. Every-

English visitors at the opening of the Suez Canal, 1869

one kept journals and after every day's shore excursion the words would appear 'Here is the steamer again and already our steamer is *home*'.

There were reassuring breakfasts of porridge, bacon and eggs, a reading room with the English papers, afternoon teas, and dressing for dinner. It was home, but in a slightly palatial style. It was dream travel: the ancient world almost daily explored, but the realities of nineteenth-century Egypt under Turkish rule held at a safe distance – at no fabulous expense. In 1873 an eighty-five-day trip of Lower Egypt, the Nile and Palestine cost only £120. Only wars could interrupt the pattern over which John Mason Cook presided – sometimes on the spot, sometimes at long range. And it was revolution and war in Egypt that stopped travel for pleasure in 1880.

GREAT BRITONS

John Mason ran Nile trips for British convalescent soldiers. Then came General Gordon on his ill-fated mission to Khartoum. Cook organised the journey of the General and his staff up the Nile as far as Korosko, whence they went on by camel, Gordon writing a note which is rightly cherished in the archives as a unique communication from a serving General to a travel agent:

Before leaving for Berber I would wish to express to you my own and Lieut.-Colonel Stewart's thanks for the admirable manner in which we have been treated while on your steamers. Your agents have also on every occasion shown themselves kind and obliging, and have in every way assisted us to the best of their ability. Hoping that I may perhaps again have the pleasure of placing myself under your guidance, I remain, ever yours truly.

Not so long after that letter was carefully filed away, John Mason Cook was summoned to a round of meetings in Whitehall where the Government was planning an expedition to extricate Gordon from Khartoum. The talks went on too long to save Gordon but Cook's job was punctual enough. 'We had to conduct the transport to the second Cataract and we conducted it almost to the hour I undertook,' he wrote.

The instructions I received were to provide for about 6000 men, with six to eight thousand tons of stores, which we had to convey from Assiout, the termination of the Upper Egyptian Railway, to Wady Halfa, the foot of the Second Cataract . . . Instead of the numbers of men I have mentioned, we have conveyed about 11,000 English and 7000 Egyptian troops, and nearly 4000 tons of stores, and have consumed nearly 24,000 tons of coal, and have conveyed a total of about 40,000 tons of coal up the river . . . We had twenty-eight large steamers between the Tyne and Alexandria; we had something like 6000 railway trucks in use between Alexandria and Boulac or Assiout, and for the military stores over 7000 railway trucks in addition . . . Then for the river work we had twenty-seven steamers employed almost day and night, and no fewer than 650 sailing boats, varying from seventy to 200 tons capacity.

Gordon died but Cook came out of the affair with his reputation so high that Steevens could declare in the once-hostile *Blackwood's Magazine* that 'the nominal suzerain of Egypt is the Sultan; its real suzerain is Lord Cromer. Its nominal Governor is the Khedive; its real governor, for a final touch of comic opera, is Thomas Cook & Son.'

The rest of the globe was not neglected. In his sixty-fourth year Thomas Cook set off with a party of nine to travel round the world. He wrote to his wife in praise of the United States:

I wish it were possible for you to see the Americans at home. I like the appearance of New York on the Sabbath, and the two congregations have been charming. I like the look of the people in their places of worship. The hotel life too is better than I expected. Four meals a day, and not a drop of drink on the tables except iced water.

A caravan of tourists posing before the Sphinx and the Pyramids

In Japan he had the best roast beef since leaving England. In India, in fine contrast to the 1841 open excursionist tubs, the party had a railway saloon carriage with sleeping berths, baths and closets which they kept for over three weeks, 'attaching it and detaching it where we liked for 2300 miles'. At Agra Thomas found 400 abstainers out of a garrison of 900. 'I was asked to give my experience of nearly forty years of abstinence in many lands and on many seas to an audience of about 500 red-jackets, and a more enthusiastic meeting on temperance I never attended.' He never could resist the good works, and these could become onerous on his hard-pressed headquarters staff, and irksome to John Mason. But this 222-day trip was also good business. A Round the World Tour became an annual event.

Soon after his return, he was deep in another good work – the first Baptist Mission in Rome – and Mrs Cook and Annie the daughter spent several weeks there preparing the new chapel for worship. Annie Cook had not lived a sheltered life. She had helped with the hotel businesses. She had travelled quite widely. Yet she was well into her thirties before she found romance. Disastrously, it was with a member of staff, one Akin Higgins. John Mason, her brother, was already at loggerheads with father, mother and poor Annie. To father, he wrote that:

GREAT BRITONS

I told them both at once that I could not have a brother-in-law member of the staff and if they were married he would have to leave our service. He appealed to me in various ways but I declined to be moved from my decision. He has left the service and I know no more than you do when the marriage is to take place.

Annie did not live to see that bitterness softened by old age. She never married Higgins, who makes his last appearance a few months after the inquest on her body. Thomas Cook had installed a new-fangled gadget, a gas water heater, in his home and poor Annie was found drowned in her bath, a victim of fumes. Higgins gave evidence that she had told him that she had lost consciousness once before in the bath. Thomas erected a Memorial Hall in the Italian style in her memory at a cost of £7000, a comfort to him in his declining years.

In 1888 Thomas was writing somewhat conciliatory letters to his son – asking a favour.

I do most earnestly desire to go up the Nile as far as Luxor or Assouan, and to enable me to do this I ask you kindly to authorise the clerk in Charge at Cairo to allot to me for the 6 March a two berth Cabin . . . [At the end of that trip he wrote:] I have met with very many of your personal friends from whom I have not heard an unpleasant word in reference to your Nile and general arrangements.

It was Thomas Cook's farewell to his beloved Egypt.

The John Mason who received this letter was at the height of his powers, a veritable giant of travel. He might have lost sight of some of the original aims to serve the working classes but, as his own sons went furthering the business to every continent, he was serving statesmen and crowned heads. W. E. Gladstone declared:

Among the humanising contrivances of the age I think notice is due to the system founded by Mr Cook, and now largely in use, under which numbers of persons, and indeed whole classes, have for the first time found easy access to foreign countries, and have acquired some of that familiarity with them, which breeds not contempt but kindness.

The high spot in John Mason's career came in the last year of his life when a musical called *The Man from Cooks* ran as a popular hit at the Gaiety Theatre, and his son Frank, who was German-speaking, worked out plans for the visit of Kaiser Wilhelm II to the Holy Land. Though John Mason was there, Frank Cook made all the arrangements and wrote proudly:

We had about one hundred and twenty Germans including the Emperor and Empress and their suites, about one hundred Turkish pashas and their suites, sent by the Sultan to do honour to the Emperor, and about twenty-five journalists, mostly English. I rode into Jerusalem in front of the State procession when the Kaiser entered the city, much to the annoyance of the German tourists who were there and did not like to see an Englishman taking the lead and having all the arrangments in hand.

THOMAS COOK & SON

Thomas Cook changed much in the Victorian world and was never a stay-at-home. Yet he remained at heart resolutely English, resolutely doing good: resolutely Baptist, though he had organised pilgrims to Mecca: resolutely temperance, though his Nile steamers were amply provided with drink.

In Leicester he had built Thorncroft, a solid mansion – without cellars – in the 1870s. It still exists, in the service of the Red Cross. Here he retired toward the end of the 1880s.

He was too old and blind to go to the grand Jubilee dinner in 1891 at the Hotel Metropole in London which was attended by royalty and celebrated by a leader in *The Times*. Fifty years since that first excursion in open tubs in 1841, the customers included the Tsar of Russia, the Shah of Persia, W. E. Gladstone, Kipling, Krupp, Vanderbilt. Toward the end of his life, in 1892, he was enjoying trips in his dreams. 'It almost nightly happens that I am engaged in my dreams in various matters of work connected with tours and travels, and I make many trips through dreamland which leave an impression upon me in the wakeful hours of the morning . . .'

His life as a practical idealist, working in equal proportions for the good of humanity and for hard cash, had dealt in dreams. He had given mobility to working people to whom it had been a dream. He had set the insular middle classes travelling. He had revolutionised travel for pleasure – and he died as he was born, a god-fearing provincial Englishman, leaving an international Empire behind him.

Cook's office at Ludgate Circus at the end of the 19th century

NIGHTINGALE

PHILIPPA STEWART

Florence Nightingale is known the world over as the Lady with the Lamp, the heroine of the Crimean War, the founder and inspiration of modern nursing. Yet she had to struggle until she was thirty-three to be allowed to do what she wanted, and was never satisfied with what she had achieved. She was born with all the advantages of money, breeding and beauty, yet she was desperately unhappy for most of her life. She had an intensely rational, scientific mind, yet was sincerely convinced that she had been 'called' by God. She was attractive to men, yet she never married, and had perhaps her most profound relationships with women. She was an invalid, bedridden for fifty years, yet from her bed she managed to organise barracks in England, sanitation in India, nurses' training schools, workhouses and district nursing; bedridden and considered on the verge of death at the age of thirty-seven, yet she lived to be ninety. Like so many products of the Victorian myth-machine, Florence Nightingale was at once more intensely human, more abrasive and more pitiable than ever her myth allowed. And therein, surely, lies her fascination.

She was born in Florence, Italy, on 12 May 1820, the second daughter of William and Fanny Nightingale. Her parents were not considered a well-matched pair. Fanny was six years her husband's senior, very beautiful, gay and fun-loving, generous to a fault, the ideal hostess. Mr Nightingale was tall and aloof, of a philosophical turn of mind, very witty when he chose to be, but, as Fanny wrote later, 'Mr Nightingale is seldom in the melting mood'. This basic incompatibility was reflected in Florence's own character, torn between sociability and introversion, natural responses and a strong sense of duty.

The Nightingales were married in 1818 and, like many of their contemporaries, decided to take advantage of the end of the long Napoleonic wars, and travel on the Continent. Their first daughter was born in Naples in 1819. In true Romantic fashion they christened her Parthenope, after the Greek name for her birthplace. This was shortened to Parthe. Their second daughter was also named after the city of her birth and, though little did they know it then, was later to inspire thousands of mothers to call their daughters by a previously unusual name, 'Florence'.

After two years on the Continent, and now with two children, the Nightingales decided it was time to return to England. Their first home was at Lea Hurst in Derbyshire; later they also acquired Embley Park near Romsey in Hampshire.

Florence had a childhood like that of any prosperous child in the early nineteenth century: two homes, one for the winter and one for the summer, with short stays in London in the spring and autumn; a host of cousins, friends and relations to stay, so that the house was always full of company; parents who were on friendly terms with many leading society figures and entertained on a lavish scale. Yet Florence was not a happy child. She had the habit, begun early in life, of writing notes about her personal feelings. Hundreds of these survive, offering a unique insight into her mind, an insight often at variance with the official pronouncements of letters and the recollections of those who knew her. In an autobiographical note she recalled: 'I was always in mortal fear of doing something unlike other people . . . I had a morbid terror of not using my knives and forks like other people when I should come out. I was afraid of speaking to children because I was sure I should not please them.' Such thoughts were not unique to Florence Nightingale; but their obvious intensity and self-absorption give an early clue to her character.

Mr Nightingale was something of a scholar, and held very definite views about what his children should be taught. A number of governesses were hired but they were never able to meet Mr Nightingale's strict criteria, and in the end he decided to teach his two daughters himself. It was an ambitious curriculum that took in Latin and Greek, mathematics and philosophy. Both the children were quick and eager learners but gradually Florence outstripped Parthe, and in time the family divided in two: Florence and her father in the library pursuing learned discussions; Parthe with her mother in the drawing-room, entertaining, arranging flowers, doing the things expected of well-brought-up girls.

In 1837 Fanny decided it was time the two girls were brought out into society. While Embley was being suitably enlarged they would all benefit from an excursion to the Continent. The house was packed up, the builders moved in, and the family prepared for a long tour. In the midst of this bustle, Florence, then sixteen, received what she believed was a call from God. She wrote in a private note: 'On 7 February 1837, God spoke to me and called me to His service.' It is hard to be rational about this sort of revelation. Florence Nightingale was not a fanciful person, and she was quite convinced that what she had heard was a real and objective voice. Years later, in 1874, she described how 'voices' had spoken to her four times during her lifetime: her first call in 1837; in 1853 before she took up her post in Harley Street; in 1854 before the Crimea; and in 1861 after Sidney Herbert's death. Whatever the 'truth', there can be no doubt that Florence herself believed in her call. For a long time she directed her life in accordance with it, and drew from it motivation and drive.

The Nightingales left England in September 1837, and were away for eighteen months, travelling across France to Italy and back. Fanny was very pleased with her daughters. They were both intelligent and good-looking, and wherever they went they were well received. Dances, balls, operas and theatres followed in quick succession. They were invited

Florence, on the left, with her sister Parthenope, c. 1836

everywhere and everyone seemed delighted by them. Florence in particular was a great success. Her demure looks concealed a quick wit.

Their return to England in April 1839 marked the start of Florence's difficulties. Her mother had all sorts of plans for her. Her success on the Continent was only a beginning. In Florence she clearly had a daughter who promised to be exceptional. In the spring of 1839 the two girls were presented at Court and spent the season in London. But instead of being happy Florence moped. She would be gay one minute, and the next morose, bad-tempered, withdrawn. Fanny couldn't understand it. The truth was that Florence was torn by internal conflict. She enjoyed being admired. At the same time she found the social life she was expected to lead intellectually intolerable. She longed for something to *do*. In 1841 she wrote to a friend: 'You ask me why I do not write something. I had so much rather live than write – writing is only a substitute for living . . . I think one's feelings waste themselves in words – they ought to be distilled into actions and into actions which bring results.'

She wanted some sort of real work, some sort of discipline, to give meaning to her life. Despairing of ever finding an outlet for her vague aspirations, she began to hate herself, blaming herself for being 'unworthy' of her call, and trying to punish herself, 'crucify' herself. She slipped into 'dreams' as an escape which soon became a habit, and as she lost touch with reality she feared she might be going mad. She was suffering from intense and undirected frustration.

Her emotional life was also going through a tumultuous phase. She had been seized by a passion for her beautiful and vivacious cousin Marianne Nicholson. 'I never loved but one person with passion in my life and that was her', she wrote in 1846. By ill-chance Marianne's brother Henry fell in love with Florence, and for four years Florence encouraged him, hoping that this would bring her closer to Marianne. Eventually Henry proposed and Florence rejected him. Marianne was furious and cut all ties with the Nightingale family, leaving Florence heartbroken. She was introduced to Richard Monckton Milnes, later 1st Lord Houghton, an eligible young bachelor, and one whose interests, in the welfare of young delinquents for example, coincided in many respects with Florence's own. Richard Monckton Milnes fell in love with Florence, and became a regular visitor to the Nightingale home. But Florence, pining over Marianne and deeply depressed about her way of life, did not respond.

Unhappy herself, she began to be obsessed by the misery of others, seeing the world in general as a bleak reflection of her own soul. 'My mind is absorbed with the idea of the sufferings of man . . . All the people I see are eaten up with care, or poverty, or disease.' The early 1840s were a cruel time for the people of England. A series of bad harvests brought widespread misery. Up at Lea Hurst for the summer, Florence found starvation and disease in plenty, and was shocked by it. 'When one thinks there are hundreds and thousands of people suffering . . . when one sees in every cottage some trouble which defies sympathy – and there is all the world putting on its shoes and stockings every morning all the same . . . death seems less dreary than life at that rate.'

She plunged into charity work, nursing the sick villagers, providing hot meals and other help for the destitute. And suddenly, unexpectedly, she found relief from her own troubles. In helping others she forgot about her torturing thoughts, and was freed from the habit of dreaming. It was an illumination. Suddenly she knew what she wanted to do, what she was happy doing, what her 'call' was. She wanted to be a nurse. 'Since I was twenty-four,' she wrote thirteen years later in a private note, ' . . . there never was any vagueness in my plans or ideas as to what God's work was for me.'

But with her intensely practical, analytical mind, Florence also realised something that few people had thought about before. Nursing was not just a matter of soothing feverish brows and handing out comforting possets. There were skills required, which were not an inherited part of every woman's nature, but could be acquired only by proper training. In a letter to her cousin Hilary she explained: 'I saw a poor woman die before my eyes this summer because there was nothing but fools to sit up with her, who poisoned her as much as if they had given her arsenic.'

At the age of twenty-four, having realised the need for training in nursing, Florence was launched on the second stage of her great battle. It had taken her five years of unhappiness and soul-searching to find out what she wanted to do. And it was another nine years, nine long bitter years, torn by strife and argument, before she was actually able to do it. She started out a malleable young girl. She ended up with a will of iron. This long period of frustration, the result of her parents' refusal to allow her to nurse, holds the key to Florence's character. If she had got her way from the beginning she might have been happy later to accept a 'normal' life. But because she was denied her wish, and denied it more unreasonably as the years went by, she hardened into steeled determination. At the same time, on the credit side, this long waiting period enabled Florence steadily to collect facts about hospitals and nursing around the world. As a result, by the time she started work she really was an expert, one of the greatest experts living, and was able to contribute to her full potential.

Florence's first plan was to study nursing at the Salisbury Infirmary where a family friend, Dr Fowler, was head physician. She had heard about the Kaiserswerth Institute in Germany, where girls of good family were employed looking after the sick in a strict religious atmosphere, and she thought she might after training set up a similar institution. When she announced her plans to her parents, however, in December 1845, they were horrified. Her mother and sister had hysterics, her father was disgusted, and Dr Fowler, frightened off by the commotion, withdrew his offer.

There was certainly justification for the Nightingales' attitude. Hospitals then were not the well-respected professional places they are today. Dickens had only too accurately portrayed Mrs Gamp as a drunken incompetent harlot. The physician of a large London hospital described how 'the nurses are drunkards, sisters and all, and there are but two nurses whom the surgeons can trust to give the patients their medicine'. Florence's parents were not prepared to see their daughter make a fool of herself by such a rash and unsuitable action, and they refused even to discuss it. Florence was shaken by their refusal. She felt she was being punished, that she was not yet pure enough to do God's work. It never occurred to her at this stage to go against her parents' wishes, although she was then already twenty-five years old.

Meanwhile she was caught in the slow trap of family life. In the summer of 1847 she looked back at what she had done the previous fortnight. 'What is my business in this world, and what have I done this fortnight? I have read the *Daughter at Home* to Father and two chapters of Mackintosh; a volume of Sybil to Mamma. Learnt seven tunes by heart. Written various letters.' 'I see so many of my kind who have gone mad for want of something to do.'

Encouraged by Lord Ashley (later Lord Shaftesbury), she began to study the government Blue Books and hospital reports, working in secret, getting up at dawn to read and make notes, before going down to be the Daughter of the House at breakfast time. Month followed month, and she felt she *was* going mad. The rift between her and her family widened. Fanny's genuine attempt to do the best by her daughter, by not allowing her to make the 'terrible mistake' of entering a hospital to work, gradually became entrenched hostility when faced by Florence's obduracy, her determination to become a nurse, and her refusal to attend parties, visit London, be pleasant, get married.

Florence was lucky that she had a number of friends who, even if they didn't fully understand her, at least cared for her enough to want to help her. In 1847, when in the depths of misery, she was invited to Rome by some family friends who hoped the trip would take her mind off her troubles. The English group wandered round the Sistine Chapel, and Florence was entranced. 'I never enjoyed any time in my life as much as my time in Rome,' she wrote. Thereafter she always had prints of the

Sistine frescoes hanging in her room. While in Rome Florence was introduced to Sidney Herbert and his wife Liz. Herbert was a leading figure on the political stage, and a notable philanthropist. Unknown to her, the jigsaw of Florence's life was beginning to take shape.

Back home, Florence's friendship with the Herberts continued. She made contact with other influential people interested in hospital reform. Slowly, as a result of assiduous study, she began to be known as an expert on hospitals. But in 1848 she was plunged again into despair when a plan to visit Kaiserswerth was cancelled because of the revolutions of that year. Florence interpreted the political scene entirely in terms of her own life, and was consumed by self-hatred. She had been stopped from going to Kaiserswerth because she was not worthy: 'My God what am I to do? Teach me, tell me. I cannot go on any longer waiting till my situation should change, dreaming what the change should be.'

She was in this unhappy state of mind when another blow fell on her. Richard Monckton Milnes proposed and insisted on a definite answer. He had been waiting for nearly seven years. Florence refused him: 'I have an intellectual nature which requires satisfaction and that would find it in him. I have a passionate nature which requires satisfaction and that would find it in him. I have a moral, an active nature which requires satisfaction and that would not find it in his life.'

For years she could not forget him; she dreamed of him coming to rescue her. But she never repented her decision. Her own destiny was more important to her now than marriage. Fanny was livid. Her great plans for Florence were turning to dust. The conflict between mother and daughter, between sister and sister, intensified, and with it Florence's guilt at the unhappiness she was causing her family.

At the end of 1850 Florence reached her lowest ebb. Looking forward and looking back, she could see no hope for herself: 'In my thirty-first year I can see nothing desirable but death . . . There is not a night that I do not lie down in my bed, wishing that I may leave it no more.' Soon after, however, her attitude began to change. Gradually she began to see herself as a victim of her family, not an oppressor, and her guilt complex turned to rebellion: 'I must expect no sympathy nor help from them . . . I must *take* some things, as few as I can, to enable me to live. I must *take* them, they will not be given to me.' At the age of thirty-one Florence was finally ready to cut herself free.

A fortnight later she had arranged to go to Kaiserswerth. As before there were furious family scenes, but Florence was no longer affected. On her thirty-second birthday, in May 1852, she was able to write to her father: 'I hope now that I have come into possession of myself . . . I hope that I may live, a thing which I have not often been able to say, because I think I have learnt something it would be a pity to waste.'

She knew now that she wanted to look after the sick, run a hospital, train nurses, and she was just waiting for the right opportunity. In 1853 it came. Liz Herbert, wife of Sidney, recommended her for the post of superintendent of the Institution for the Care of Sick Gentlewomen in Distressed Circumstances, which was moving to new premises in Harley Street, London. After prolonged negotiations Florence was appointed. At last she was launched on her career. Returning from a holiday in Paris she refused to stay with her family, but instead took rooms in Pall Mall until her quarters in Harley Street were ready.

It was quite some task organising the rambling, shambling Institution, whose ways had been allowed to grind into inefficient ruts for many years. In the way she set about it Florence showed all the talents that were to stand her in good stead in the Crimea. Her genius was of a decidedly unromantic nature. She realised that good nursing above all meant good and efficient organisation. She arranged the kitchen and the supplies system, the pharmacy and the dispensing, installed lifts and bells. In a letter to her cousin Hilary she described how she was living 'in an ideal world of lifts, gas, baths, and double and single wards'. She was in her element. On 1 January 1854 she wrote: 'I have never repented nor looked back, not for one moment. And I begin the New Year with more true feeling of a happy New Year than I ever had in my life.'

But there was by this time a certain iciness, a certain steel about Florence Nightingale. Mrs Gaskell, who visited Lea Hurst in October 1854, noticed it:

She has no friend – and she wants none. She stands perfectly alone, half-way between God and His creatures. She used to go a great deal among the villagers here, who dote upon her . . . She will not go among the villagers now because her heart and soul are absorbed by her hospital plans, and she says she can only attend to one thing at once. She is so excessively soft and gentle in voice, manner and movement that one never feels the unbendableness of her character when one is near her.

Florence stayed at Harley Street for a year, and by the end of that time was already growing restless with the limited scope it offered. Her quarterly report to the Governors in August 1854 noted:

I consider that my work is now done, that the Institution has been brought into as good a state as its capabilities admit. I have not effected anything towards the object of training nurses – my primary idea in devoting my life to Hospital work . . . I therefore wish, at the close of the year for which I promised my services, to intimate that . . . I may retire, if . . . I meet with a sphere which is more analogous to the formation of a Nursing School.

Meanwhile, fate had taken a hand. The jigsaw of Florence's life was

Severe conditions hampered army supplies: wagons bogged down on the road from Balaclava to Sebastopol

about to fall into place. On the other side of Europe a small peninsula called the Crimea was the centre of a major war, in which the two great superpowers of Britain and France were involved in a bid to save Turkey from Russian encroachment.

The army that the British government sent to the Crimea was an army that had not fought since Waterloo forty years before. Yet so smart were the uniforms, and so ingrained in public consciousness was the memory of the victory at Waterloo, that the people of Britain had no doubt that their army would be victorious. In April 1854 they watched complacently as the first proud detachments of troops marched out. They were sure they would be back before Christmas. They did not know, and even if they had known they would not have realised the significance of the fact, that the men who marched so proudly by were standing up in the only clothes they had; that they were being sent to fight overseas, in a rough and primitive country, with no proper supplies, no proper equipment. The summer wore on. In the hot and dusty land troops fell sick from cholera and dysentery. Their packs were abandoned to lighten their load. In the first skirmishes of the war, at the Battle of Alma, they fought valiantly, but they were already hampered by the fatal combination of sickness and lack of supplies.

However, although the army had not improved since Waterloo, communications had. In William Howard Russell, an explosive Irishman and reporter for *The Times*, the British public had their first war correspondent. Daily over their breakfast tables they could read now about the bravery of troops, and the blunders of army administration, in graphic and persistent detail. Russell was particularly incensed at the treatment of the wounded. After the Battle of Alma in October 1854 he reported:

It is with feelings of surprise and anger that the public will learn that no sufficient preparations have been made for the care of the wounded . . . the men must die through the medical staff of the British Army having forgotten that old rags are necessary for the dressing of wounds.

Worse was to follow. A few days later Russell wrote:

There are no dressers or nurses to carry out the surgeons' directions, and to attend on the sick during the intervals between his visits. Here the French are greatly our superiors. Their medical arrangements are extremely good, and they have also the help of the Sisters of Charity . . . these devoted women are excellent nurses.

The British public was shocked by Russell's revelations. The idea that the French were better organised was particularly wounding. Why had the British no Sisters of Mercy? As Secretary of State for War, responsible for the financial administration of the army, Sidney Herbert was under attack. As upset as anyone, and anxious to do something immediately, he turned to the only person he knew capable of organising a party of British nurses, Florence Nightingale. On the previous day Florence herself had written to Sidney Herbert asking permission to do just that. The jigsaw was complete.

There was a clear need to act quickly and Florence set about gathering her nurses at once. It was no easy task. As she had already discovered while in Harley Street, there were few good trained nurses about. However, on 21 October, just a week after the second of Russell's articles, the motley party of thirty-eight nurses embarked. They travelled across France to Marseilles where Florence, ignoring the protestations of plenty put forward by the authorities, bought supplies of various sorts. They then caught a boat to Constantinople. The weather was rough, and Florence, a bad sailor, was seasick most of the way. They arrived in Constantinople on 4 November 1854. Across the water, on the Asiatic shore, they could see the tall, grim building of the Barrack Hospital at Scutari where they were due to begin work.

The first impression of Scutari was not very inviting. The bloated carcass of a horse lay riding the tide, worried by a pack of mangy dogs. Up the hill to the hospital the path was steep and rutted. The Barrack Hospital itself looked bleak and inhospitable. As its name suggests it had once been a Turkish barracks, built on four sides round a central square. Three sides had been turned into a hospital by the simple expedient of laying mattresses along the dank corridors. The fourth side had been gutted by fire and was for the time being unusable. The Nightingale party were assigned six small rooms, one of which was still occupied by the corpse of a dead Russian general, whose white hairs liberally adorned the floor. The nurses soon discovered other drawbacks to their new home. There were no beds for them to sleep on, no food for them to eat. The water supply was limited to a pint per head a day – which had to cover all contingencies.

Florence soon realised something else about the hospital: the medical staff were not pleased to see her or her nurses. Working as they were under tremendous pressure, and smarting from the attacks made by *The Times*, they felt that her arrival cast a slur on their reputations. Dr John Hall, Chief of Medical Staff, who was based at Balaclava across the Black Sea from Scutari, had bravely but unwisely told the government that all was well with the hospital, its supplies and equipment. Having declared

The Barrack Hospital at Scutari, 1854

William Howard Russell, correspondent of The Times, *writing a dispatch in his tent. Florence Nightingale can be seen in the background*

Sick and wounded soldiers lying in the mud at Balaclava harbour, awaiting the agonising crossing to the hospital, 1855

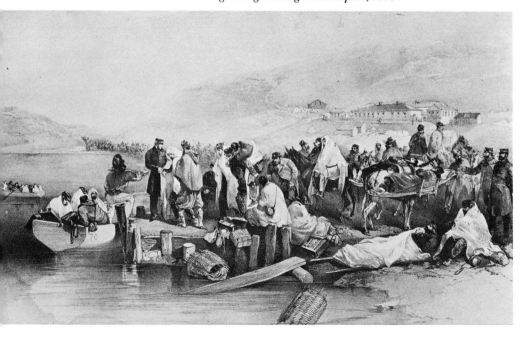

this so adamantly he had no desire to lose face, and throughout Florence's time in the 'East' he fought hard to discredit her work.

From the beginning Florence realised that she would achieve nothing if she antagonised the medical men in charge of the hospital. So she instructed her nurses that they were to do nothing without the specific authorisation of a doctor, not even to fetch a glass of water for a dying man, or smooth the pillow of a fever patient. Instead she set them to sorting linen. It was a policy which required immense self-discipline, and the nurses grumbled among themselves. But Florence was aware of the wider issues at stake. In the letter which Sidney Herbert had written asking her to undertake the work, he had spelled out what she later took as her main objective in coming to Scutari: to reconcile the army to the presence of female nurses. 'If this succeeds,' he wrote, 'a prejudice will have been broken through, and a precedent established, which will multiply the good to all time.' It was in this light, as the organiser of an experiment that had to prove itself successful, rather than as an angel of mercy soothing the wounded soldiery of Britain, that Florence Nightingale saw her mission.

The actual fighting was taking place across the Black Sea from Constantinople and Scutari, in the Crimean peninsula. As the winter drew in the weather worsened. The men on the battlefield began to suffer not only from wounds but from sickness brought on by the cold, and by inadequate food and clothing. To get to hospital they were carried down the steep slopes to the harbour at Balaclava, by that time a morass of mud and putrefaction, where they were loaded into ships bound for Scutari. The crossing was often choppy, and the men's agonies great. By the time they arrived at the hospital, any injuries they might have sustained were generally surpassed by their weakness from the journey.

The Battle of Balaclava had been fought on 25 October, and the casualties began to arrive soon after Florence had settled into the hospital. 5 November saw the Battle of Inkerman, a British victory but at terrible cost. The numbers of sick and wounded multiplied rapidly, and they poured into Balaclava. William Howard Russell described their journey down the hillside:

They formed one of the most ghastly processions that ever poet imagined . . . With closed eyes, open mouths and ghastly attenuated faces, they were borne along two by two, the thin steam of breath visible in the frosty air alone showing that they were alive. One figure was a horror, a corpse, stone dead, strapped upright in its seat . . . Another man I saw with raw flesh and skin hanging from his fingers, the raw bones of which protruded into the cold, undressed and uncovered.

The first sick transports reaching Scutari were not even expected, and they continued to flood in at such a rate that the hospital system broke down. The harassed medical men, deprived of even the most basic necessities, turned to Florence Nightingale, suddenly realising that here was one person who had the money, and the power, to make good some of the deficiencies, and moreover who was prepared to take action without delay. Nurses started to assist at operations, provide warm food and drinks, stuff sacks with straw to make more mattresses, anything at all that would keep the hospital from utterly seizing up.

Conditions were desperate. On the heights above Balaclava the Russian winter was getting into its stride, with storms, and sleet that cut like a knife. More and more shiploads of sick poured into Scutari, in rags and covered in lice, starving and diseased. By the end of November 1854 the official administration of the hospital had collapsed, and Florence became, in her own words, 'a kind of General Dealer: in socks, shirts, knives and forks, wooden spoons, tin baths, tables and forms, cabbages and carrots, operating tables, towels and soap, small tooth combs, precipitate for destroying lice, scissors, bedpans, and stump pillows.' She organised her nurses to scrub the wards and corridors, ensured that the latrines were emptied, and when 500 more sick were announced, managed to find enough Turkish workmen to repair the fourth side of the hospital which had been destroyed by fire. In fact for six months, almost single-handed, Florence Nightingale ran the purveying of the hospital.

But that was only a small part of her work. In a letter dated 14 November 1854, she gave an idea of the strain on the hospital staff:

We had but half-an-hour's notice before they began landing the wounded. Between one and nine o'clock we had the mattresses stuffed, sewn-up, laid down – alas! only upon matting on the floor – the men washed and put to bed, and their wounds dressed . . . twenty-four cases died on the day of landing. The dysentery cases have died at the rate of one in two.

The work was continuous. In between receiving the sick and organising the hospital, Florence somehow found time to write innumerable letters: she wrote for the soldiers, she wrote for her nurses; she kept up a constant flow of long and detailed reports to Sidney Herbert, full of plans for wide-ranging reforms. At the same time she had to sort out problems with her nurses, and liaise with the authorities; superintend the care of the wounded, and nurse the dying. In that first winter she estimated that she witnessed over 2000 deaths. At night she went her rounds of the wards:

As I went among the newly wounded there was not one murmur, not one groan, the strictest discipline – the most absolute silence and quiet prevailed . . . These poor fellows bear pain and mutilation with an unshrinking heroism which is really superhuman, and die, or are cut up without a complaint.

FLORENCE NIGHTINGALE

In his official account of the war, the historian Kinglake put aside his normally pedestrian prose to describe Florence at work:

The magic of her power over men was felt in the room – the dreaded, the bloodstained room – where operations took place. There perhaps the maimed soldier, if not yet resigned to his fate, might be craving death rather than meet the knife of the surgeon, but when such a one looked up and saw that the honoured Lady in Chief was patiently standing beside him – and with lips closely set and hands folded – decreeing herself to go through the pain of witnessing pain, he used to fall into the mood of obeying her silent command and – finding strange support in her presence – bring himself to submit and endure.

One result of this was that a strange, strong bond grew up between Florence Nightingale and the ordinary soldiers of the army. Florence was deeply impressed by the soldiers' stoicism, their dumb courage, their loyalty. It was a bond of almost mystical proportions which Florence treasured for the rest of her life, and which inspired much of her later work. And the soldiers in turn loved Florence:

What a comfort it was to see her pass even. She would speak to one, and nod and smile to as many more; but she could not do it all you know. We lay there by hundreds; but we could kiss her shadow as it fell and lay our heads on the pillow again content.

Meanwhile the conditions and the death-rate were worsening all the time. By January 1855 there were 12,000 men in hospital and only 11,000 in the trenches before Sebastopol. The battle casualties were falling, but the death-rate was on the increase. The wards had become infested with fever, and the men in them no longer expected to live.

Back home in England there was a groundswell of indignation and anger. The brave heroes whom Russell had described charging at Bala-clava, fighting against overwhelming odds at Inkerman, were now being left to die from disease and neglect. The government was embarrassed, and sought to ease the situation by setting up two Commissions of Enquiry. One, the McNeill and Tulloch Commission, was to examine the system of supplies for the British Army in the Crimea. The other, the Sanitary Commission led by a Dr Sutherland, was to investigate the sanitary state of the hospitals. From each Florence acquired lifelong colleagues. But she believed it was the Sanitary Commission that actually saved the British Army. They landed at Scutari in March, and began work immediately. Some of their discoveries were hair-raising. They found, for example, that the entire water supply for the Barrack Hospital was pas-sing through the carcass of a horse. The building itself was standing in filth. The water was stored in tanks in the courtyard, built next to tem-porary privies which had to cope with the needs of thousands of men

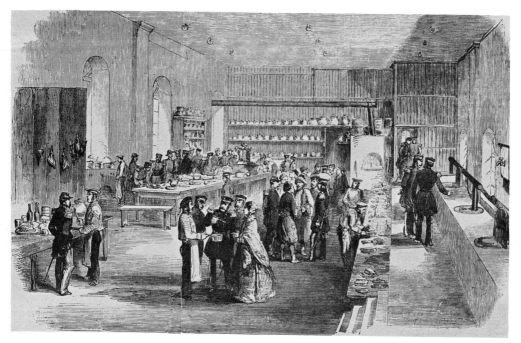

Alexis Soyer's kitchen at Scutari: his enormous teapot stands on the far table

suffering from diarrhoea. The hospital abounded in rats, and the very walls were steeped in dirt and excrement. The Commission began to clean the sewers and limewash the walls, and at once the death-rate fell.

At the same time conditions for the patients inside the hospital were improving. In March 1855 an eccentric French chef, Alexis Soyer, arrived at his own expense to take charge of the Barrack Hospital kitchens. He had devised ways of cooking food in large quantities that were both delicious and nutritious – two qualities the hospital food had not previously enjoyed. He invented an enormous teapot which could make tea for fifty men at a time. And as a public relations exercise he organised a dinner party for the ambassador and his wife, at which he served delicious dishes made from army rations. Florence Nightingale was quick to recognise Soyer's genius, and became his friend. 'Others,' she said, 'have studied cookery for the purpose of gourmandising, some for show. But none but he for the purpose of cooking large quantities of food in the most nutritive and economical manner for great quantities of people.'

Now that the Barrack Hospital seemed to be on a sounder footing, Florence decided it was time she visited some of the hospitals across the

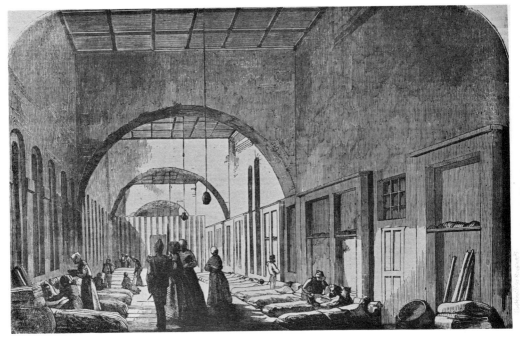

A ward in the Barrack Hospital at Scutari, 1854

Black Sea in the Crimea itself. On 5 May 1855 she arrived in Balaclava. After a quick tour of the ramparts, she got down to work, but not for long. Within two days she was ill with fever, and for several weeks lay between life and death. The long hours of work, the inadequate food, the hardships she had endured were taking their toll. Feverish as she was, Florence continued to cover sheet after sheet of paper with scarcely legible scribbles; she couldn't be persuaded to put down her pen. Reliving in vivid nightmare the past months she was convinced her room was full of people: demanding supplies, advice, information. This illness marks a clear turning point in Florence Nightingale's Crimean career. Although she recovered, her health was broken, and so was her self-confidence. Never again was she to feel strong, elated or secure. She continued to work hard but from this time on was haunted by a sense of failure.

On her return to the Barrack Hospital in August 1855 Florence would not rest. She was grimly determined to reform the whole British Army. Against the opposition of the authorities she opened a small reading room for convalescent soldiers. She fought for facilities for the men to remit money to their wives and children at home; £71,000 was sent home in less than six months. She opened a recreation room, furnished with news-papers and writing materials. Schools and classes were organised, plays put on.

Throughout the summer and autumn of 1855 Florence laboured, often in opposition to the medical authorities who, now that conditions inside the hospital had improved, no longer felt that her presence was necessary. Aunt Mai, her father's sister, travelled out to Scutari to help her, and reported back:

The public generally imagine her by the soldier's bedside . . . how easy, how satisfactory if that were all. The quantity of writing, the quantity of talking is the weary work, the dealing with the mean, the selfish, the incompetent . . . Suppose you could see us now . . . Flo at her large table covered with papers, I at my little table with my tiny work. We speak not a word. The wind roars, the rain patters. I don't think Flo is conscious of the bluster. I never saw a mind so continuously concentrated on her work. Is it a mind that belonged to some other planet? For it does not seem adapted to the human frame, though it has forced that frame to obedience. She continually writes till one or two, sometimes till three or four; has in the last pressure given up three whole nights to it. You would be surprised at the temperature in which she lives, she who suffers so much from cold . . . She has attained a most wonderful calm. No irritation of temper, no hurry or confusion of manner ever appears for a moment.

But that calm was on the surface only. The weakness that would turn her into an invalid was already making itself felt. After a difficult inter-view she would collapse on the sofa in a state of exhaustion. More impor-tant, her self-confidence was undermined. 'The victory is lost already,' she told Aunt Mai. In January 1856 the McNeill and Tulloch Commission into the supplies for the British Army presented its report to Parliament. The report confirmed what Florence Nightingale had already said in private: that the reason for the lack of supplies was the bureaucratic inefficiency of the system. But instead of accepting the report the gov-ernment did an extensive whitewashing job, and indeed promoted many of those, including Dr John Hall, who had been named in it as culpable. Florence was appalled:

I who saw the men come down through all that long dreadful winter, without other covering than a dirty blanket and a pair of old regimental trousers, when we knew the stores were bursting with warm clothing, living skeletons devoured by vermin, ulcerated, hopeless, speechless . . . Can we hear of the promotion of the men who caused this colossal calamity, we who saw it? Would that the men could speak who died in the puddles of Calamita Bay!

Her depression bordered on despair as she saw all she had worked for crumbling around her. Dr John Hall refused to accept her authority over the nurses in the Crimea and would not allow her to direct them. A confidential report was sent to the War Office accusing her of mismanagement. Her own nurses were turning against her, and the medical staff had reverted to their old antagonism.

At this low ebb Florence unexpectedly received support from a source she had known had existed, but which she had never thought would manifest itself. The common people of Britain had taken Florence Nightingale, the story of the 'Lady with the Lamp', to their hearts. She became a national heroine, immortalised in the memories of Crimean survivors. Doggerel verses were composed in her honour, songs and hymns sung. A penny version of her life story was printed and sold by the thousand. She was depicted in china and pottery and porcelain, in innumerable prints and engravings. The romantic vision of her with a lamp in her hand, soothing the brow of a wounded soldier, was born and thrived. It ignored the sordid reality of the Crimea, the hard work and harsh conditions. But it was a powerful vision, and one which has survived more or less intact to this day.

Her friends at home profited from it to hold a public meeting, in November 1855, 'to give expression to a general feeling that the services

The impact of the 'Nightingales' on public opinion is shown in this contemporary cartoon

of Miss Nightingale in the Hospitals of the East demand the grateful recognition of the British people'. A substantial fund was set up to enable her, at some future date, to 'establish and control an institute for the training, sustenance and protection of nurses paid and unpaid'. Even the Queen, 'to mark her warm feelings of admiration', presented her with a brooch designed by Prince Albert.

But Florence Nightingale remained unmoved. She disliked the razzamatazz about her name, the 'buz fuz' as she called it. She wrote to her mother, 'My reputation has not been a boon in my work'. She was touched by the devotion of the common people, but was more concerned about the problems still facing her. Throughout her time in the 'East', she had been hampered by an inadequate description of her authority. Her original appointment stated that she was to be 'Superintendent of the Female Nursing Establishment of the English General Hospitals in Turkey'. Thereafter the two words 'in Turkey' were taken by some officials to mean that she had no jurisdiction over the hospitals in the Crimea, although that had not been the original intention. As a result, although the Crimean hospitals were in a state of disarray, her authority was flouted, both by nurses and by officials who disliked her influence. For a long time Florence had been fighting for proper recognition. At last, on 16 March 1856, she had an almost unique honour. 'General Orders' sent out from the War Office and posted up in every barrack and mess spelled out her sole and entire responsibility for all the nurses in the military hospitals of the army. But it was really too late. The war was over and peace talks had started in Paris.

Florence again travelled to the Crimea to try and put the hospitals there into some sort of order. On 29 April peace was declared, but she felt no exultation. From Balaclava she wrote to Sidney Herbert: 'Believe me when I say that everything in the Army (in point of routine *versus* system) is just where it was eighteen months ago . . . *Nous n'avons rien oublié ni rien appris* . . . In six months all these sufferings will be forgotten.'

Back at Scutari she dragged herself through her final duties, tidying up the hospital, sending home her nurses, each one with a personal 'character': 'Mrs Tainton – came out in April 1855. Perfectly sober and respectable, good and active nurse. Trustworthy and truthful. But much given to thoughts of marriage, which is inconvenient in a Hospital Nurse in this field, perhaps more so than in a young lady in a drawing room.' For some she arranged a free passage home, others she assisted herself. None of them was to be 'thrown off like an old shoe'.

Florence herself, however, remained utterly depressed. Her health had suffered a great deal, her mind perhaps even more so. In private notes, as in her youth, she began to pour out the bitterness in her heart: 'Oh my poor men who endured so patiently, I feel I have been such a bad mother to you to come home and leave you lying in your Crimean graves. Seventy-three per cent in eight regiments – who thinks of that now?' She left Scutari on 28 July 1856, travelling incognito with her Aunt Mai as Mrs and Miss Smith. The whole of England was waiting to give her a hero's welcome, but she slipped undetected to London and arrived at Lea Hurst on 7 August. Parthe wrote to a friend: 'She is come home as you will see – so quietly that save ourselves no one knew it . . . She looks well in the face and seems well for the first few hours of the morning, but then she seems wearied out for the rest of the day.'

Looking back at Scutari, Florence was overwhelmed by a sense of despair, and also of urgency. She was aware of the public interest in the Crimea, and knew that to make any permanent changes she had to strike while the iron was hot. There was so much that needed to be done, only she knew how much, and only she could do it. 'I stand at the altar of murdered men, and while I live I fight their cause,' she wrote in a private note. 'If I could only carry *one* point which would prevent *one* part of the recurrence of the colossal calamity, then I should be true to the brave dead.'

So, exhausted as she was, and close to collapse, she got down to work. She was certain that a repetition of the Crimean catastrophe could be avoided only by a thorough overhaul of the entire army system. She planned to ask for a Royal Commission 'to examine the sanitary condition, administration, and organisation of barracks and military hospitals and the organisation, education and administration of the Army Medical Department', and was invited to put her views to the Queen and Prince Albert at Balmoral. The Prince described how 'she put before us all the defects of our present military hospital system and the reforms that are needed. We are much pleased with her; she is extremely modest.' 'I wish we had her at the War Office,' wrote the Queen. But the War Office itself was most reluctant to instigate the sort of wide-ranging inquiry Florence had envisaged, and procrastinated month after month.

The delay was a torment to Florence. She made herself ill dwelling on the disaster that, as always, she felt she alone appreciated:

No one can feel for the Army as I do. These people who talk to us have all fed their children on the fat of the land and dressed them in velvet and silk while we have been away. I have had to see my children dressed in a dirty blanket and an old pair of regimental trousers, and to see them fed on raw salt meat, and nine thousand of my children are lying, from causes which might have been prevented, in their forgotten graves.

After pressure from all sides, the Commission was finally set up in May

Sidney Herbert

1857, under the chairmanship of Sidney Herbert. It sat throughout the long hot summer of 1857, interviewing witnesses, taking notes, preparing recommendations. The strain on Florence was tremendous. She was in weak health already, and she was working day and night, travelling, interviewing, writing, writing, writing. She was living at the Burlington Hotel, and her task was not made easier by the presence of her mother and sister, who were determined to stay in London for as long as she did.

Ten years later the wounds of that summer were still raw. Writing in 1867 Florence described how 'the whole occupation of Parthe and Mamma was to lie on two sofas and tell one another not to get tired by putting flowers into water . . . It is a scene worthy of Molière where two people in tolerable and even perfect health lie on the sofa all day, doing absolutely nothing, and persuade themselves and others that they are the victims of self-devotion for another who is dying of overwork.' The result of this was that Florence cut herself off completely from her family. For many years after she refused to see either Fanny or Parthe, and would be seized by a fit, palpitations, extreme weakness, whenever they threatened to come near. Their place at her side was taken by her Aunt Mai, whose own life and family were largely sacrificed to Florence.

As if the work of the Commission was not enough, Florence was at the same time preparing a digest of her thoughts on the army medical system, *Notes on Matters Affecting the Health, Efficiency and Hospital Administration of the British Army*, which she completed also in the summer of 1857. It is a volume of nearly 1000 closely-printed pages crammed with facts and statistical tables. She used her experiences in the Crimean War as the basis for a wide-ranging discussion, and coined a phrase which became the reformers' battle cry: 'Our soldiers enlist to death in the barracks.'

Only too soon Florence became aware that her task would not end with the publication of the Report of the Royal Commission. In July she scribbled a note to herself: 'Reports are not self-executive', and she repeated the phrase again and again. Her work would only be done when the recommendations of the report had all of them been realised. She was still haunted. She could have no rest.

In August 1857 the report was finished, and Florence collapsed. She had eaten no solid food for weeks, was utterly exhausted, and was generally thought to be close to death. She retired to Malvern, and her obituary notice was prepared for the newspapers. When she returned to London in September she did so as an invalid. Henceforth she stayed indoors, mostly in bed, and her strength such as it was was reserved solely for work. For she could not stop working. In November 1857 Aunt Mai reported: 'Mr Herbert for three hours in the morning, Dr Sutherland for four hours in the afternoon, Dr Balfour, Dr Farr, Dr Alexander

Florence in 1858. Her health had been broken by the war

interspersed . . . Flo is working double tides, labouring day after day until she is almost fainting.' Florence drove herself so hard because, like all the people around her, she was convinced she had at the most a few months to live. By the end of 1857 she was ready for death. She drew up her will, she agreed the arrangements for her funeral. To Sidney Herbert she wrote: 'I hope you will not regret the manner of my death.'

But Florence did not die; indeed she was to live for another half-century and more, outlasting most of her contemporaries. However, the fact that for a long time she was convinced she was about to die yet continued to drive herself on, meant that she was not at all sympathetic to the illnesses of people around her: what could their sufferings compare with her own, she who was on the very verge of death? This was at its most obvious in her attitude towards Sidney Herbert. In attempting to put through all the reforms suggested by the Royal Commission, and in particular the complete reform of the War Office, Sidney Herbert had bitten off more than he could chew. He achieved a great deal: the Army Medical School was set up, for example, under his direction, and barracks were greatly improved. But his health was weak, and the attempt to tackle so many insurmountable problems at once weakened him further.

Sidney Herbert's eventual death in 1861 provides a convenient milestone from which to look back at the extent of Florence's work in the five years after the Crimea. It is quite bewildering to try and grasp the vast number of things she was involved in. There was her work with Sidney Herbert for the army, the Royal Commission, the struggle to get its recommendations put into effect, and the effort of collecting and collating the statistics needed for her *Notes* on the health of the army. But there was so much more.

A hospital ward in the 1880s, built to Florence's specifications: light and airy, to promote recovery and prevent re-infection

Before she went to the Crimea Florence had been recognised as an authority on hospitals, and on her return she was consulted frequently about hospital construction. She was a strong believer in the pavilion idea, where the hospital is divided into a number of separate blocks: 'The object sought is that the atmosphere of no one pavilion or ward should diffuse itself to any other pavilion or ward, but should escape into the open air as speedily as possible, while its place is supplied by the purest obtainable air from outside.' In 1859 she published her views in *Notes on Hospitals*, which begins with the immediately arresting statement: 'It may seem a strange principle to enunciate as the very first requirement in a Hospital that it should do the sick no harm.' In the book Florence explained how the high hospital mortality rate could be reduced by better drainage, better ventilation and higher standards of hygiene. She did not believe in germs, in fact refused ever to accept their existence, but thought that 'miasms' (polluted air) were the cause of cross-infection. She also devised a system of hospital statistics and a standard classification of diseases.

In the same year, 1859, she published an immensely readable little book, intended for 'every woman in England', *Notes on Nursing: what it is and what it is not*. The book shows a sympathetic understanding of both the nurse's and the patient's viewpoint, and includes practical hints on hygiene in the home, food, light, bedding and baby care. Many of the ideas advocated were at the time quite revolutionary, and the book caused a minor sensation when it appeared. It quickly sold out, was reprinted several times, and is still worth reading today.

Amidst her toil the only relaxation Florence allowed herself was a form of metaphysical speculation. She began by redrafting a manuscript she had written in 1851, designed to provide a new religion for the 'artisans of England'. At the end of 1859 she had copies privately printed under the title *Suggestions for Thought*, which she sent anonymously to a number of well-known figures to obtain their comments. John Stuart Mill was enthusiastic. A copy was sent to Benjamin Jowett, later Master of Balliol; although he did not recommend publication, he became as a result of this introduction one of Florence's closest friends.

For a long time the Nightingale Fund, standing at £45,000, was a millstone around Florence's neck, and on several occasions she tried to relinquish responsibility for it. Eventually however she was persuaded to use it for the purpose for which it had been intended, to set up a training school for nurses. Having had dealings with St Thomas's Hospital in London, and conceived the highest regard for its matron Mrs Wardroper, she decided to base the school there. There was some opposition from within St Thomas's, and from the medical world in general, but the school opened in July 1860 with fifteen probationers. As with her nurses in the

Crimea, Florence was obsessed by the importance of these first 'Nightingale nurses'. The whole future of nurses' training could depend on them; she wanted to know everything about them, to supervise their every thought. Probationers had to keep a daily diary which Florence read at the end of each month. Mrs Wardroper and she exchanged long and anxious letters about their achievements and the development of their character.

Then, at the very moment Florence was beginning to see some results from her work, she received a cruel blow: Sidney Herbert's health broke down. The hard years of unconvivial toil had taken their toll. Florence rebelled violently against the idea of losing her main support and mouthpiece in government circles, and tried hard to persuade him that he was not as ill as he thought: 'I hope you will not judge too hardly of yourself from these doctors' opinions . . . I am not going to bore you with a medical lecture. But I don't believe there is anything in your constitution which makes it evident that disease is getting the upper hand. On the contrary.' Exhorted by Florence and by his wife, Sidney Herbert continued working to the bitter end. In June 1861 he collapsed. Florence was implacable, refused to forgive him for his desertion of the cause: 'How perfectly ineffective is a reform unless the reformer remains long enough at the head to MAKE IT WORK,' she told him witheringly. 'No man in my day has thrown away so noble a game with all the winning cards in his hands.' On 2 August 1861 Sidney Herbert died, with his last dying words, his last thoughts, for Florence: 'Poor Florence . . . poor Florence, our joint work unfinished.'

Florence was overwhelmed by his death; she really had not expected it: 'He takes my life with him. My work, the object of my life, the means to do it, all in one depart with him . . . And I alone of all men "most deject and wretched" survive . . . I am sure I meant to have died.' All her old bitterness, her rancour and despair returned. 'I feel like the Wandering Jew – as if I *could not* die.' She blamed God, she blamed the world. As always she felt that nobody else's grief could compare with her grief:

I have lost all. All the others have children or some high and inspiring interest to live for – while I have lost husband and children and all. I am glad to end a day which never can come back, gladder to end a night, gladder still to end a month . . . Now hardly a man remains (that I can call a man) of all those I have worked with these five years. I survive them all. I am sure I did not mean to.

And yet Florence Nightingale lived on, for nearly fifty years after Sidney Herbert's death, and achieved a tremendous amount. The ramifications of her interests were immense; the sheer quantity of work she got through from her bed, usually alone and often unhappy, is staggering. Very soon after his death she began serious work on what was to be one of her abiding interests for almost thirty years: India. She had already involved herself in India in 1859, when she had campaigned for a Royal Sanitary Commission. She had drafted a *Circular of Enquiry* which was sent to every military station, asking for details of sanitation, water supply, living conditions and rate of mortality. Now she was asked to prepare a digest of these station reports, and in so doing acquired a knowledge of India that was without equal. Her *Observations* were published in 1862 and for the first time highlighted the extent of the problem in India. Statistics she produced showed that for years the annual death-rate in the Indian Army had been some 69 per 1000: 'A company out of every regiment has been sacrificed every twenty months.' Drunkenness was endemic. The water supplies were universally contaminated. No drainage existed 'in any sense in which we understand drainage'. Even worse were the conditions endured by the native troops. Florence realised that if she was to improve the health of the British troops in India, she would have to start by improving the level of sanitation in the country as a whole: 'The salvation of the Indian Army must be brought about by sanitary measures everywhere.'

Her position in Indian affairs was extraordinary. She had never been to India, yet was consulted regularly by men who had lived there all their working lives. Year after year she toiled, collecting facts and marshalling them into order. Her prodigious memory served her well. Viceroys and governors called on her before leaving England to be briefed on salient details and what action to take. She maintained her interest in the welfare of the Indian people and campaigned for irrigation schemes to combat starvation, new forms of taxation, the right of Indians to enter the Civil Service.

Yet India was not all her work. In the years after Sidney Herbert's death she became involved in the workhouse system and Poor Law reform, district nursing and childbirth statistics. As ever, she threw herself into all of these with tremendous energy, writing endless letters, absorbing immense quantities of facts and figures, continually struggling to improve standards. She was recognised around the world as an inspiration and an example. Henri Dunant, the founder of the International Red Cross, said of her: 'Though I am known as the founder of the Red Cross and the originator of the Convention of Geneva, it is to an Englishwoman that all the honour of that Convention is due. What inspired me . . . was the work of Miss Florence Nightingale in the Crimea.' On a more humble note, Mr Farnall, a Poor Law inspector, described how 'from the first I had a sort of fixed faith that Florence Nightingale could do anything'.

Her 'Nightingale nurses' were a continuing source of interest. She tried to know them all personally, invited them to stay, and kept in touch with most of them long after they had left the school, and were spreading her

A group of nurses from St Thomas's Hospital at Claydon House, 1886. Behind Florence stands her brother-in-law Sir Harry Verney

standards around the world. She was involved in the controversy over whether there should be a register of qualified nurses. Florence fought hard against registration, believing that it was a nurse's attitude towards her work that was crucial. 'It is not the certificate which makes the Nurse or the Midwife. It may *un-make* her. The danger is lest she let the certificate be *instead* of herself, *instead* of her own never ceasing going up higher as a woman and a Nurse.'

One of the few things Florence Nightingale did not concern herself with, however, strange as it may appear, was a cause that was agitating most informed women from the 1860s onwards, women's rights. Florence had no time for the feminist fight, whether it was for the right to enter the professions, or to vote. Indeed she was bitter about women's attitudes: 'My doctrines have taken no hold among women. Not one of my Crimean following learnt anything from me . . . It makes me mad the "Women's Rights" talk about the "want of a field" for them – when I know that I would gladly give £500 a year for a Woman Secretary.' She herself had found plenty to do, and enough influence to capture the ear of the government. She could not see that she was any different from other women, except that she worked harder; and she was exasperated by attempts to emulate men: 'To do things just because men do them!' she wrote contemptuously – when there was so much that women could do, and do well, and didn't.

Year after year Florence toiled at her various interests. She was an invalid, she lived alone, and for a long time she sacrificed all ordinary pleasures to her work, conserving her energies for the one great task of reform. She seldom left her bed, and saw no visitors except by appointment – even royalty were turned away at the door. Her sole means of communication with the outside world was via Dr Sutherland. She had met him first in the Crimea, where he was a member of the Sanitary Commission. Thereafter he served on most of the commissions which she instituted, and became her mouthpiece and go-between. Yet Florence never really liked him; she appreciated his ability but he irritated her. He would turn up late for meetings, be vague about facts, was conveniently deaf. She developed a system of communicating with him by scribbling notes on odd scraps of paper: 'What has become of the eight copies of the Indian Report? Where is Barbadoes? Where are the three Registrar General papers?' 'There's fish for you at one.' Despite her irritation she relied on him, however, and increasingly as the years went by.

In due course it became obvious that Florence was not on the verge of death, but she remained convinced she was very ill. Time after time in her letters she complained: 'I am ill'; 'I have been an overworked invalid for 25 years and an just now scarcely able to write'. She corresponded with her friends and family, but used her weakness as a shield against them: she would not allow them to visit her or to interfere with her work. In 1858 her sister Parthe had married Sir Harry Verney, owner of the beautiful Claydon House. In later years Florence grew closer to her family; she cared for her mother in her old age, was a regular visitor to Claydon, and nursed Parthe when her arthritis was crippling. But the reconciliation was never complete, and she continued to resent any demands her family made on her.

For a long time indeed, she felt unfairly persecuted by the world in general. The bitterness and anguish of her youth remained with her right into middle age. At forty-five she was writing: 'It would be idle to wish me, or perhaps anyone who has seen this world as I have, a "happy New Year".' In the same year she moaned to Jowett: 'I lost my serenity some years ago, then I lost clearness of perception, so that sometimes I did not know whether I was doing right or wrong for two minutes together – the horrible loneliness.' At forty-seven she felt herself 'not only a shattered wreck of what I was but a phantom among phantoms.' At fifty-four she was still desperately depressed: 'Am I she who once stood on that Crimean height? "The Lady with a Lamp shall stand." The lamp shows me only my utter shipwreck.'

Her friendship with Benjamin Jowett brought her some serenity. He tried to make her appreciate the enormous amount she had achieved, despite the reversals. 'There was a great deal of romantic feeling about you twenty-three years ago,' he wrote in 1879, 'when you came home from the Crimea . . . And now you work on in silence, and nobody knows how many lives are saved by your nurses in hospitals; how many thousand soldiers who would have fallen victims to bad air, bad drainage and ventilation, are now alive owing to your forethought and diligence; how many natives of India . . . have been preserved from famine, oppression and the load of debt by the energy of a sick lady who can scarcely rise from her bed.' Jowett also helped her in other ways. He asked her advice over a new translation of Plato, and later suggested she should compile a book of extracts from devotional writers of the Middle Ages. Florence found relief in these tasks. She had always been interested in metaphysical questions, and was something of a mystic. In 1874 she expressed what was perhaps her creed in life: 'Religion is not devotion, but work and suffering for the love of God . . . Where shall I find God? In myself. That is the true Mystical Doctrine. But then I myself must be in a state for Him to come and dwell in me.'

Florence also derived great comfort from the company of cats. Unlike humans they were quiet, they did not jangle her frayed nerves, and they provided an endless source of interest. In later years she always had two or three cats in her room. In 1890 she wrote to a young friend:

I learnt the lesson of life from a little kitten of mine, one of two. The old cat comes in and says, very cross, 'I didn't ask you in here, I like to have my Missus to myself!' And he runs at them. The bigger and handsome kitten runs away, but the littler one *stands her ground*, and when the old enemy comes near enough kisses his nose, and makes the peace. That is the lesson of life, to kiss one's enemy's nose, always standing one's ground.

Gradually the acerbity died away. The great battles had been fought, and lost or won, but they were over. In her old age Florence was happier than at any time in her life: 'There is so much to live for. I have lost much in failures and disappointments, as well as in grief but, do you know, life is more precious to me now in my old age.' She found pleasure in the company of young people: her relatives at Claydon, the nurses at the Nightingale School. She corresponded with her nurses in the most exaggerated terms. One probationer was addressed as 'Goddess-Baby', another as 'the Pearl'. She took parties of nurses down to Claydon for holidays, sent them food parcels when they were overworked, and flowers to brighten their rooms.

Slowly her amazing faculties faded, and the confines of her world drew in. In 1901 she went blind. The world continued to honour her. In 1907 she was awarded the Order of Merit. 'Too kind, too kind,' she murmured as it was brought to her bedside.

The end came on 13 August 1910. She was buried in the family grave at East Wellow churchyard; her memorial reads simply: 'F.N. Born 1820. Died 1910.' She was at rest at last.

The last authorised photograph of Florence Nightingale

BURNS

DAVID DAICHES

All over the world, Scotsmen get drunk on his birthday. And they sing this song, that Burns wrote about himself:

> There was a lad was born in Kyle,
> But what na day o' what na style,
> I doubt it's hardly worth the while
> To be sae nice wi' Robin.

Kyle is the central district of Ayrshire, the county in south-west Scotland where Burns was born on 25 January 1759. Robin he called himself, and his friends called him that, or Rabbie, or Rab. He would have loved to know that he would be celebrated riotously and at the same time with scrupulous ritual, for he loved both riot and ritual. But what an extraordinary thing, for a poet to be taken to a nation's heart in this passionate way.

His father, William Burns, was a gardener first, then rented a farm in order to improve his children's prospects. If his father had continued as a gardener, Burns later wrote, 'I must have marched off to be one of the little underlings about a farm-house; but it was his dearest wish and prayer to keep his children under his own eye till they could discern between good and evil'.

It was a rough life. Burns was born in the village of Alloway (now part of the city of Ayr), in a clay cottage his father had built with his own hands. When he was six his father took the farm of Mt Oliphant, a few miles to the east, and found it a pretty ruinous bargain. These were bad days for farming in Ayrshire: rents of farms had risen enormously in expectation of improvements that had not yet been carried out. Mt Oliphant was seventy acres of ill-drained clay soil, and the inflated rent was £40 a year. In 1777 the family moved to a larger farm ten miles away – Lochlie, 130 acres at the even more inflated rent of one pound a year per acre. Both farms proved ruinous bargains, and William died in 1784 worn out and bankrupt. Robert and his younger brother Gilbert had helped him work the farm – arduous physical labour on an insufficient diet: it gave Robert the rheumatic heart disease from which he eventually died at the age of thirty-seven.

Robert's younger brother Gilbert later remembered what life was like at Lochlie:

To the buffetings of misfortune, we could only oppose hard labour and the most rigid economy. We lived very sparingly. For several years butcher's meat was a stranger in the house, while all the members of the family exerted themselves to the utmost of their strength, and rather beyond it, in the labours of the farm. My brother at the age of thirteen assisted in threshing the crop of corn, and at fifteen was the principal labourer on the farm, for we had no hired servant, male or female. . . .

Birthplace of Burns at Alloway

Though times were difficult, William Burns, with his passion for education so characteristic of the Scottish peasantry, saw to it that his sons were well educated in standard English. He and four of his fellow farmers jointly hired a very genteel young man called John Murdoch to teach their children. Murdoch used an anthology of English literature which contained passages from Shakespeare, Milton and Dryden as well as from eighteenth-century poets. Burns became especially fond of Thomas Gray and his famous Elegy. He knew Thomson and Shenstone too. And the prose work of Addison was also represented in the anthology. And of course he was thoroughly grounded in the Bible and in biblical history as it was then understood. There was something else too. Murdoch trained these Scottish peasant children to write a highly formal standard English – elegant, correct, at times somewhat stilted, but always clear and precise.

And they were taught to appreciate English literature from Shakespeare to his own day. Burns was even taught some French, and eventually acquired a smattering of Latin. No illiterate peasant here.

But what about Scotland and Scottish literature? Scottish formal education at this time was oriented entirely towards England – one of the many results of historical developments since James VI of Scotland became also James I of England in 1603 and since the Union of Scotland with England in 1707. Yet there was a Scottish literature – a splendid older Scottish poetry written when Scots was a vigorous literary language in its own right, not just a series of regional dialects, as it had become by Burns's time. And there was a vigorous Scottish folk literature swirling all around him. Burns later wrote about this:

In my infant and boyish days, I owed much to an old Maid of my Mother's, remarkable for her ignorance, credulity and superstition. She had, I suppose, the largest collection in the county of tales and songs concerning devils, ghosts, fairies, brownies, witches, warlocks, spunkies, kelpies, elf-candles, dead-lights, wraiths, apparitions, cantraips, giants, inchanted towers, dragons and other trumpery. This cultivated the latent seeds of Poesy.

Years later Burns was to produce in 'Tam o' Shanter' a splendidly lively poem based on folklore associated with Alloway Kirk.

As a youngster, and indeed all his life, Burns alternated between moods

Lochlie farm; engraving of the early 19th century

109

of depression and of high gaiety – almost manic-depressive in fact. And he alternated too between the formal English poetry he read in books and the Scottish folk songs and folk legends he heard all around him. But what made him a poet anyway? This is what he said himself: 'I never had the least thought or inclination of turning Poet till I got once heartily in Love, and then Rhyme and Song were, in a manner, the spontaneous language of my heart.'

He was not quite fifteen when he wrote his first poem, 'Handsome Nell', a love song set to a folk tune, like so many of his later songs. In style and idiom, it is in the folk manner; but its language is an effective mixture of standard English and Scots, the Scots giving it freshness and local authenticity.

Burns entered this poem in a Commonplace Book he began to keep in April 1783. This Commonplace Book gives a fascinating picture of young Burns – proud, moody, ambitious, alternating between moods of self-conscious morality and deep melancholy and happy, lilting liveliness. It makes clear too that he already saw himself as a poet, and one who would be remembered.

But what sort of poetry was he going to write, this young Scottish peasant with his English-oriented education and his roots among the working country people of Ayrshire? He could turn out imitations of neo-classic English poetry with considerable facility, and this is what many minor and mostly forgotten poets of Scotland were doing at this time. But something in Burns knew that this was not good enough. He was moved towards older Scottish poetry by discovering a modernised version of the fifteenth-century patriotic Scottish poem *Wallace*, and then he discovered the Scots poems of Robert Fergusson, the brilliant young Edinburgh poet who had died in the public Bedlam of that city in 1774 when he was only twenty-four. This was decisive. 'I strung anew my wildly-sounding rustic lyre with emulating vigour.'

The early years at the farm of Lochlie between 1777 and 1780 were probably the happiest ever spent by the Burns family as a whole. After that things went from bad to worse on the farm. Robert made many friends in the nearby villages of Tarbolton and Mauchline, and with some of them he founded the Tarbolton Bachelors' Club in November 1780. Burns loved gatherings of cronies; he loved drinking with them; he also loved the rituals of formally constituted societies. Later he became a Freemason and always enjoyed Masonic ritual. The Tarbolton Bachelors' Club was a debating society in which Burns could argue about his favourite grievances – they concerned the differences between the classes, the fact that while as a youngster he could play with the children of the gentry, when they grew up they would look down on him simply because they had more money.

The Tarbolton Bachelors' Club gave him a sense of belonging: it also gave him an audience, which was important for him. He started writing verse letters to members – the verse letter was a poetic form he came to handle with remarkable brilliance. He also strutted and posed a bit before them. He was a rebel, a show-off, a restless, ambitious, flirtatious, exhibitionist young man.

He still had gloomy moods, but looking back on this period in 1787 he remembered it as a period of gaiety:

My life flowed on much in the same tenor till my twenty-third year. Vive l'amour et vive la bagatelle, were my sole principles of action . . . Poesy was still a darling walk of my mind, but 'twas only for the humour of the hour. I had usually half a dozen or more pieces on hand; I took up one or other as it suited the momentary tone of the mind, and dismissed it as bordering on fatigue. My Passions when once they were lighted up, raged like so many devils, till they got vent in rhyme; and then conning over my verses, like a spell, soothed all into quiet.

And what sort of poems was he writing at this time? Some were gloomy and histrionic, in standard English. Others were not:

> A country lad is my degree,
>   An' few there be that ken me, O;
> But what care I how few they be,
>   I'm welcome ay to Nanie, O.
>
> My riches a's my penny-fee,
>   An' I maun guide it cannie, O;
> But warl's gear ne'er troubles me,
>   My thoughts are a', my Nanie, O.

'Warl's gear', the world's goods, are repudiated in favour of the passionate moment with his girl. This little song, written to an old tune 'My Nanny, O', is the first of many that show Burns's capacity to grasp the realised moment of experience. Here is its last stanza:

> Come weel come woe, I care na by,
>   I'll tak what Heav'n will sen' me, O;
> Nae ither care in life have I,
>   But live, an' love my Nanie, O.

He did the same thing with another song, written to another old tune, this time called 'Corn Rigs are Bonie'. The original old song survived only in a rather indecent chorus. Burns wrote his own words, and ends with a characteristic outburst in which everything is concentrated on the moment of passionate physical love:

I hae been blythe wi' Comrades dear;
I hae been merry drinking;
I hae been joyfu' gathrin' gear;
I hae been happy thinking;
But a' the pleasures e'er I saw,
Tho' three times doubled fairly,
That happy night was worth them a',
Amang the rigs o' barley.

These poems are not written exclusively in Scots, but with an easy mixture of Scots and English, an English tipped with Scots. His more solemn and gloomy poems are more purely English.

Burns also made contact with an old Scottish tradition of animal poems, and in 'The Death and Dying Words of Poor Mailie' (a sheep), as well as in 'Poor Mailie's Elegy' he shows a splendid humour as well as poetic craftsmanship of a high order. In the Elegy he uses an old Scots stanza that he was to use often again – so often that it has become known as the 'Burns stanza'. It is best known in 'To a Mouse'.

On their father's death Burns and Gilbert managed to extricate themselves from his bankruptcy and, with the help of a friendly liberal-minded lawyer Gavin Hamilton, rent from him the farm of Mossgiel, half-way between Mauchline and Lochlie. They moved there in the early spring of 1784. The rent was £90 per annum for 118 acres – more reasonable than the pound per acre that William had paid at Lochlie.

His father's death freed Robert to indulge his sexual passions more freely. In May 1785 Elizabeth Paton, who had been a farm servant in the Burns household, bore him his first illegitimate child. Elizabeth did not expect marriage. Burns's mother cheerfully undertook to rear the baby. And Burns welcomed his daughter with a burst of affectionate boasting:

Thou's welcome, Wean! Mischanter fa' me,
If thoughts o' thee, or yet thy Mamie,
Shall ever daunton me or awe me,
My bonie lady;
Or if I blush when thou shalt ca' me
Tyta, or Daddie.

Burns was not unique in his sexual adventuring. It was extremely common at this time for country girls to bear illegitimate children, so much so that the Kirk had developed a special procedure to take care of the situation. The errant parents had to receive public rebuke in church. The father, having received and accepted the rebuke, was given a certificate recognising him as a bachelor, thus relieving him of any obligation to marry the girl. But the public rebuke in church was extremely humiliating, and there were cases when the girl was driven to suicide.

Burns, however, was always proud of his girls and proud of his children, illegitimate as well as legitimate. When Jean Armour, whom he eventually married, was about to bear his child (or twins, as they proved to be) he put into her mouth a poem that combines feminine joy in sexual surrender with feminine concern as a mother. It is a remarkably daring, and a remarkably characteristic, poem:

> *O wha my babie-clouts will buy?*
> *O wha will tent me when I cry?*
> *Wha will kiss me where I lie?*
> *The ranting dog, the daddie o't.*

It's an odd thing. Burns loved domesticity, he loved what he called in one poem 'the happy fireside clime, wi' weans and wife' which he regarded as the most permanent kind of felicity. And, unlike the true rake, he proudly and tenderly associated physical love-making with its consequences (in those days before the pill) – children. One can't imagine Byron, for example, doing this. Or Shelley, for that matter. He could write poems of physical passion, poems of protective tenderness, poems where love is regarded from the woman's point of view, bawdy poems, poems of male friendship, and bitter satirical poems. He took human relationships for what they were. Perhaps that is the clue to the special kind of affection in which he is held?

Burns was now the head of the household, known throughout the countryside as 'Rab Mossgiel', according to the Scottish habit of calling a man by the name of his farm. His friendship with Gavin Hamilton, who admired his poems, gave him confidence. Hamilton was in revolt against the sterner aspects of Scottish rural Calvinism and encouraged Burns to revolt against the strict discipline of the Kirk. He made other friends, important among whom was Robert Aiken, 'Orator Bob', the genial and eloquent Ayr lawyer some twenty years older than the poet. Aiken became both friend and patron and, with Hamilton, served as link between the struggling farmer and the genteel world.

Burns wrote and circulated among his friends some brilliant poetic satires on hard-line Calvinist characters in the Kirk. The finest of these is 'Holy Willie's Prayer', in which, as Burns put it, 'a rather oldish batchelor Elder in the parish of Mauchline . . . famed for that polemical chattering which ends in tippling Orthodoxy, and for that Spiritualised Bawdry which refines a Liquorish Devotion' is supposed to be overheard at his prayers. In his prayers Holy Willie unconsciously damns the creed he professes by revealing the hypocrisy it breeds:

O thou that in the heavens does dwell!
Wha, as it pleases best thysel,
Sends ane to heaven and ten to hell,
A' for thy glory!
And no for ony gude or ill
They've done before thee.

I bless and praise thy matchless might,
When thousands thou hast left in night,
That I am here before thy sight,
For gifts and grace,
A burning and a shining light
To a' this place. . .

The poem damns the Calvinist view that a tiny minority are predestined to election and salvation while the vast majority are predestined to damnation, regardless of anything they do, for all acts of fallen man are evil in the sight of God. It damns this creed dramatically, by revealing what it does to a man who professes it. Of course it is unfair, but this is satire.

A more affectionate kind of satire on the Kirk is 'The Holy Fair', a marvellously funny description of one of the great outdoor communion services then common in the west of Scotland, written with great dexterity in an old Scottish stanza form. Here the scene is richly Breughelesque, with the teeming congregation, the rival preachers, the drinking, the rival claims of the flesh and the spirit. A young man while listening to a sermon gradually slips his arm around his 'ain dear lass' sitting beside him:

Wi' arm repos'd on the chair back,
He sweetly does compose him;
Which by degrees, slips round her neck,
An's loof upon her bosom   [*loof* = hand]
Unkend that day.

How monie hearts this day converts,
O' Sinners and o' Lasses!
There hearts o' stane, gin night are gane
As saft as ony flesh is.
There's some are fou o' love divine;
There's some are fou o' brandy;
An' mony jobs that day begin
May end in Houghmagandie
Some ither day.

This is how the poem ends [*fou* means *drunk; houghmagandie* is *fornication*].

These poems, considered scurrilous by the orthodox, were circulated in manuscript among his friends. So were the verse letters he wrote to several of them, splendidly vital poems, where the poet begins by setting the scene – the time of year, the state of the countryside, himself writing – then goes on to pull back the camera, as it were, widening and widening the scene until he reflects on life as a whole, and then moves back in again on himself writing in the farm kitchen, to sign off at the end wittily and gracefully. At the centre of many of these verse letters stands some element of Burns's creed of humane egalitarianism.

In 1785 Burns fell in love with Jean Armour, daughter of a master mason of Mauchline. Jean responded eagerly to Robert's advances, and before long the two were deeply involved with each other. Soon Jean was pregnant. They both wanted marriage, and in Scots law consummation followed by a declaration by both parties of an intention to marry constituted a legal marriage. But Robert had counted without Jean's parents, who were furious at having their daughter mixed up with a man they considered a blasphemous rebel. They would rather see her give birth to an illegitimate child than married to such a character. So they prevailed on her to retract her consent. Robert was furious. While he suffered the pangs of a rejected lover, the injury to his pride was greater than the injury to his passion. (Pride and passion, he once wrote, were the two major elements in his character.) He turned for comfort to Mary Campbell – the Highland Mary of Burns legend. We know little about her. She died in October 1786 and the terrible pangs of guilt felt by Robert at her death suggests that she may have died in giving birth to his child. But this has never been proved.

He was in deep trouble. The 'holy beagles' of the Kirk, as he called them, were after him for fornication. Jean Armour's father was after him for money to support Jean's as yet unborn child. To make matters worse, he still loved Jean. He wrote to his friend David Brice:

Never man lov'd, or rather ador'd, a woman more than I did her: and, to confess a truth between you and me, I do still love her to distraction after all, tho' I won't tell her so, tho' I see her, which I don't want to do. . . . I have tryed often to forget her: I have run into all kinds of dissipation and riot, Mason-meetings, drinking matches, and other mischief, to drive her out of my head, but all in vain: and now for the grand cure: the Ship is on her way home that is to take me out to Jamaica; and then, farewel dear old Scotland, and farewel dear, ingrateful Jean, for never, never will I see you more.

In July 1786 he made his peace with the Kirk by doing (as Jean too had done) public penance for fornication and got his certificate as a bachelor. His desperate decision to emigrate to Jamaica to escape the financial claims of Mr Armour (who threatened to have him thrown in prison) and the pangs of his own conscience may not have been wholly serious; for ship after ship left without Burns on board. He had something else in mind.

In early April 1786 Burns had concluded arrangements with the Kilmarnock printer John Wilson for bringing out a volume of 'Scotch Poems'. In July he assigned the copyright of the book to Elizabeth Paton, for the support of his illegitimate daughter by her. On 3 September Jean bore him twins, and Burns used his 'feelings as a father' to postpone and finally abandon his plan to go to Jamaica. But by now there was a more cogent reason for his staying in Scotland. 'Poems, Chiefly in the Scottish Dialect, by Robert Burns' had been published on 31 July.

The success of the book was immediate. It swept the countryside. The Reverend George Lawrie, a liberal-minded minister in the Parish of Loudon a few miles from Mossgiel, sent a copy to Edinburgh to Dr Blacklock, the blind poet and literary critic with a great reputation among that city's *literati*, as Edinburgh's men of letters and intellectuals liked to call themselves. Blacklock wrote back to Lawrie expressing his own enthusiasm for the poems and reporting that such famous critics as Professor Dugald Stewart shared his opinion. Lawrie gave the letter to Gavin Hamilton, and Hamilton showed it to Burns.

It was the turning point of Burns's career. He heard the call of Edinburgh, the city of the eighteenth-century Scottish Enlightenment, the city of distinguished critics and historians and philosophers. A city where speculations about the origins of poetry and the nature of primitive poetry had been going on for some time. So were reflections on the nature of the 'natural man'. Here was – they thought – an untutored rustic writing authentic poetry under no inspiration but that of his own feelings. A remarkable case history indeed!

This was of course nonsense. Burns was not the 'Heaven-taught ploughman' that the novelist and critic Henry Mackenzie hailed him as in his review of the Kilmarnock volume. But he had posed as one in his carefully written preface, to catch the attention of the *literati*. In that preface he said of himself: 'Unacquainted with the necessary requisites for commencing Poet by rule, he sings the sentiments and manners, he felt and saw in himself and his rustic compeers around him, in his and their native language.'

This is to do injustice to his own carefully-cultivated verse craftsmanship, his training in English poetry, his careful putting together of standard English and rustic Scots in order to produce a poetic language which was both rooted in a local situation and angled at a wider audience.

It was on 27 November 1786 that Burns set out from Mauchline for Edinburgh, riding a horse borrowed from his friend George Reid of Barquarie. It was a two-day journey. At the end of the first day he reached the farm of Covington Mains, near Biggar, where a Mr Prentice made what Burns called 'a most agreeable little party' for him.

Burns reached Edinburgh on the afternoon of the next day, and proceeded to Baxter's Close, Lawnmarket, where his old friend John Richmond now lived, in a room rented from a Mrs Carfrae. He shared Richmond's room and bed for eighteen pence a week.

Baxter's Close, like all the Edinburgh 'closes', was a narrow street flanked by high flats. It was in the heart of the Old Town of Edinburgh, running off the Lawnmarket, which is at the western end of the wide thoroughfare that runs along the ridge joining the Castle on the west with Holyrood Palace on the east. By this time Edinburgh's New Town was well under way, the elegantly-planned development to the north of the valley of the drained North Loch. But the ordered gentility of the New Town was not for Burns – not at this stage anyway.

In Edinburgh Burns was fêted and lionised and given masses of bad advice. On 7 December he wrote to Gavin Hamilton:

For my own affairs, I am in a fair way of becoming as eminent as Thomas a Kempis or John Bunyan; and you may expect henceforth to see my birthday inserted among the wonderful events, in the Poor Robin's and Aberdeen Almanacks, along with the black Monday, and the battle of Bothwel bridge. My Lord Glencairn and the Dean of Faculty, Mr H. Erskine, have taken me under their wing; and by all probability I shall soon be the tenth Worthy, and the eighth Wise Man, of the world. Through my Lord's influence it is inserted in the records of the Caledonian Hunt, that they universally, one and all, subscribe for the second edition.

In contrast to the confusion of the old Town, where Burns began his time in Edinburgh, the New Town was emerging, orderly and elegant

Baxter's Close,
from a
19th-century
watercolour

ROBERT BURNS

He kept his sense of humour and his sense of proportion. He knew that to the people of Edinburgh he was but a nine days' wonder.

On 16 December he wrote to Robert Aiken:

You will very probably think . . . that a hint about the mischievous nature of intoxicated vanity may not be unreasonable, but alas! you are wide of the mark. Various concurring circumstances have raised my fame to a height which I am absolutely certain I have not merits to support; and I look down on the future as I would into the bottomless pit.

About the same time he wrote to the Reverend William Greenfield, minister of St Andrew's Church at Edinburgh and a literary man whom Burns soon came to admire greatly:

Never did Saul's armour sit so heavy on David when going to encounter Goliath, as does the encumbering robe of public notice with which the friendship and patronage of some 'names dear to fame' have invested me . . . I am willing to believe that my abilities deserved a better fate than the veriest shades of life; but to be dragged forth, with all my imperfections on my head, to the full glare of learned and polite observation, is what, I am afraid, I shall have bitter reason to repent.

Mrs Alison Cockburn, a poetess prominent in Edinburgh society, wrote: 'The man will be spoiled, if he can spoil, but he keeps his simple manners, and is quite sober.'

Dr Robert Anderson, a medical man who had turned from medicine to literature, later gave a vivid impression of his meeting Burns in Edinburgh at this time:

I was struck with his appearance, so different from what I had expected in an uneducated rustic. His person, though neither robust nor elegant, was manly and pleasing; and his countenance, though dark and coarse, uncommonly expressive and interesting. With an air of keen penetration and calm thoughtfulness approaching to melancholy, the usual attendant on genius, there was a kind of stern pride and supercilious elevation about him not incompatible with openness and affability, which might perhaps be properly termed a strong consciousness of intellectual excellence. His dress was plain, but genteel, like that of a farmer of the better sort: a dark-coloured coat, light-figured waistcoat, shirt with ruffles at the breast, and boots, in which he constantly visited and walked about the Town. He wore his hair, which was black and thin, in a queue, without powder. Such was Burns, as he stood before me as I entered the drawing-room.

No words can do justice to the captivating charms of his conversation. It was even more fascinating than his poetry. He was truly a great orator. Though his knowledge in many instances was superficial, yet he conversed on every subject in a manner that evinced the strongest marks of genius, and acuteness, combined with the most powerful sallies of wit, sarcasm, and satire. With acuteness of intellect, which might sometimes be termed shrewdness, he possessed a still more useful talent, Good Sense, which enabled him instantly to discern what was right or wrong in literature, morality, and the general affairs of the world . . .

119

Drawing of Burns by Skirving

But Dr Anderson recognised faults in Burns too. Like others in Edinburgh, he resented Burns's air of independence, and thought he should have shown more deference to the views of the socially superior people he met:

The pride of genius or the affectation of singularity often led him wantonly to oppose received opinions, and pertinaciously to maintain the most unreasonable positions. His prejudices, personal, political, and religious, were strong, and misguided the rectitude of his judgment; and his temper was uncertain and capricious, being influenced by the impulse of passion or the whim of the moment.

With his deeply felt passion for equality, Burns fiercely resented any suggestion that a fool should be deferred to because of his rank or wealth. He gave offence many times in Edinburgh by making this view clear. He also disliked being regarded as a kind of rustic freak, to be shown off at dinner parties, and sometimes sharply refused invitations if he thought they were given with this motive.

He was in fact in a very difficult situation. Renowned critics joined in advising him to write conventional English verse, to drop his Scots idiom, to employ classical mythology and other supposedly elegant ornaments to poetry. It shows his remarkable confidence in the nature of his own genius that he only rarely succumbed to this advice.

Perhaps the best known reminiscence of Burns in Edinburgh is that of Sir Walter Scott, who later told his son-in-law and biographer J. G. Lockhart an account of his meeting Burns at the house of Dr Adam Ferguson when he himself was only sixteen:

There was a strong impression of sense and shrewdness in all his lineaments: the eye alone, I think, indicated the poetical character and temperament. It was large, and of a cast which glowed (I say literally *glowed*) when he spoke with feeling or interest. I never saw such another eye in a human being, though I have seen the most distinguished men of my time. His conversation expressed perfect self-confidence, but without the least intrusive forwardness; and when he differed in opinion, he did not hesitate to express it firmly, yet at the same time with modesty.

Burns had chosen the poems for the Kilmarnock volume with care. He had omitted the stronger ecclesiastical satires and those poems he thought might give offence. Even so, it was a remarkable collection. It included that witty and subtle social satire 'The Twa Dogs' – a conversation between a rich man's dog and a poor man's dog which manages to attack with humorous liveliness everything that Burns disliked about the idle rich. 'The Holy Fair' is here, its geniality outweighing the implied satire. The two poems on Mailie the sheep. A fine selection of verse letters. The show-piece – 'The Cotter's Saturday Night', a slow-moving, emotionally weighted picture of a Scottish tenant farmer at home. The charming and wholly unsentimental 'To a Mouse', where the fellow feeling for the little creature is linked to an awareness of common suffering. And one of my own favourites, 'To a Louse, On Seeing one on a Lady's Bonnet at Church', where with affectionate ironic humour he restores to common humanity the proud young lady sitting in church in her new bonnet, unaware that a louse is crawling on its back.

Among the poems not included is the remarkable Cantata, as he called it, which we know as 'The Jolly Beggars' but which Burns entitled 'Love and Liberty'. In a series of songs set to known tunes, linked by passages of narrative verse, Burns shows a group of outcasts, beggars, drop-outs and social misfits assembled at a pub in Mauchline, singing and tippling and announcing their defiance of society. It is a work of pure anarchism, and it represents one strain – and one strain only – in Burns's character. This is how the last song ends:

Life is all a variorum,
We regard not how it goes;
Let them prate about decorum
Who have character to lose.

A fig for those by law protected!
Liberty's a glorious feast!
Courts for Cowards were erected,
Churches built to please the Priest.

No wonder he dared not submit it to the censures of the *literati*.

Yet, in spite of the inevitable strains, he behaved with dignity and made a good impression. Professor Dugald Stewart later remembered:

His manners were then, as they continued ever afterwards, simple, manly, and independent; strongly expressive of conscious genius and worth; but without anything that indicated forwardness, arrogance, or vanity. He took his share in the conversation, but not more than belonged to him; and listened with apparent attention and deference, on subjects where his want of education deprived him of the means of information.

But Stewart added, significantly:

If there had been a little more of gentleness and accommodation in his temper, he would, I think, have been still more interesting; but he had been accustomed to give law in the circle of his ordinary acquaintance; and his dread of anything approaching to meanness or servility, rendered his manner somewhat decided and hard.

Mauchline, c. 1840

ROBERT BURNS

It never occurred to any of the *literati* who commented on Burns's defensive hardness in conversation that this may have been the simple result of his having a better mind than they had. For Burns happened to arrive in Edinburgh between two phases of the city's Golden Age, the age of David Hume, the great philosopher who died in 1776, and the age of Walter Scott, still only a boy. There were many critics and scholars and men of letters in Edinburgh society in the winter of 1786-7, but not a really first-rate intellect among them. Ten years before and twenty years later it would have been a different story.

He found relief from the pomposities of the *literati* in the friendship of William Nicol, a coarse and irascible Latin master at the High School of Edinburgh. Burns didn't mind his coarseness, and relished his wit and gaiety. With Nicol he spoke a racy Scots, and the only letter of Burns that survives written entirely in Scots is one to Nicol. Burns also joined the Crochallan Fencibles, a drinking club which met in Anchor Close, not far from Baxter's Close where he was staying. Here he found an atmosphere very different from that of the drawing-rooms of the *literati*. Bawdy songs and jokes and a great deal of drinking.

Burns's main objects in going to Edinburgh were to arrange for a second edition of his poems and to get a job in the Excise service, then regarded as an appropriate way of enabling a poet to earn a living. He was successful in the first objective, and what is known as the Edinburgh edition of Burns's poems was published on 21 April 1787. He was unsuccessful at this time in getting an Excise job. The *literati* thought that it was appropriate for a peasant poet to stay on the farm. Burns himself was not anxious to continue farming: he knew all too well the hardships and difficulties of farming in Ayrshire in those days.

The Edinburgh edition did not include much of significance that was not already in the Kilmarnock edition: the best new poem in it is 'The Brigs of Ayr', a dialogue between the old and new bridges of Ayr written in an old Scottish tradition but at the same time combining English with Scottish influence. The Edinburgh edition also included 'To a Haggis', ritually recited at every Burns Supper, and the well-known song 'Green Grow the rashes, O', which he had composed some years before but had not thought worth including in the Kilmarnock volume. Like so many of Burns's songs, it was written to a known tune and based on an old chorus. There was an old bawdy version of the song that Burns once quoted to a correspondent in discussing his sexual adventures.

An Edinburgh banker called Patrick Miller who had recently bought the estate of Dalswinton in the valley of the Nith near Dumfries offered Burns the lease of a farm on it. Burns hesitated to take up the offer. He was restless and unsettled, and didn't quite know what he wanted. He was aware, too, that his popularity with the *literati* would not last for ever. In February 1787 he wrote to Mrs Frances Dunlop, an elderly Ayrshire widow with whom he had formed an almost filial relationship:

The novelty of a Poet in my obscure situation, without any of those advantages which are reckoned necessary for that character, at least at this time of day, has raised a partial tide of public notice which has borne me to a height, where I am absolutely, feelingly certain my abilities are inadequate to support me; and too surely do I see that time when the same tide will leave me, and recede, perhaps, as far below the mark of truth.

This did not mean that he had lost his self-confidence as a poet. He knew exactly what his poetic talents were and how he wanted to use them. He wanted to progress from being the bard of Ayrshire to being the poet of Scotland. In January his fellow Freemasons at the Grand Lodge of Scotland had toasted him as 'Caledonia's Bard, Brother Burns', and he relished that.

But he had a long way to go before he could justify this title. He wanted to get to know Scotland better, to familiarise himself with its countryside, its patterns of work and play, its folk songs and traditions. In April 1787 he met James Johnson, a self-educated lover of Scottish songs who had invented a cheap process for printing music by using stamped pewter plates. Johnson was proposing to publish a collection of Scottish songs and enlisted Burns's help. Burns responded with enormous enthusiasm, taking this as a mandate not just to collect and pass on any fragments of old Scottish folk song he could find, but to do something much more: to re-create these fragments into new songs which, while in the genuine folk tradition, were essentially Burns's own work. What he did for Johnson, and later for another music publisher George Thomson, was to breathe new life into the scattered fragments of Scottish folk song – old choruses, bits of verses, bawdy fragments, tunes with titles but no words, and so on. He took no money for this, considering it a patriotic duty. And the vast majority of songs which he re-worked he never claimed as in any sense his own. We still do not know the precise extent to which he was involved in many of the hundreds of songs he sent to Johnson and Thomson. Of course many were wholly his own; many, we know, were re-workings of old songs or filling out of old choruses. But many of the most famous songs we know as by Burns – including 'A Red, Red Rose' and 'Auld Lang Syne' – he never claimed as his own, but passed on as old songs he had discovered.

Burns took a series of trips to familiarise himself with Scotland. First he visited the Border country, so rich in historical and literary tradition. He set out from Edinburgh on 5 May 1787, and twice crossed the Border into

England before returning to Mossgiel four days later on 9 May.

Now that Burns had returned from Edinburgh a national hero, Jean Armour's parents changed their view of him. A man who had been fêted by the gentry in Edinburgh was certainly fit for their daughter to marry. But Burns was revolted by what he called 'their mean, servile compliance' and claimed that he had no intention of marrying Jean.

In June he was off on another exploratory tour of his native land – this time in the Argyllshire Highlands. He enjoyed himself. He returned to Mossgiel in July, and visited Jean and the twins she had borne him the previous September. Though he still declared he would not marry her, he could not resist taking up with her again, and she does not seem to have objected in the least. Jean became pregnant again, and bore him girl twins the following March: both died soon afterwards.

He went back to Edinburgh in August 1787, to try and collect the money due him for the Edinburgh edition of his poems. (He didn't get all he was owed until March 1789.)

He still felt that his destiny to be Scotland's poet required him to familiarise himself further with Scotland. On 25 August he set out from Edinburgh on a Highland tour with William Nicol. They went by Linlithgow, Stirling, Crieff, Aberfeldy, Blair Atholl, through Strathspey to Aviemore and then on to Inverness. Everywhere he went Burns observed and listened; noted the landscape with a farmer's eye; heard work songs, love songs, stories and legends of local beauties. From Inverness he went east by Forres to Elgin, along the southern shore of the Moray Firth to Banff, then down the east coast from Peterhead by Aberdeen and Stonehaven to Montrose, then back to Edinburgh by way of Dundee, Perth and Kinross. They crossed the Firth of Forth at Queensferry.

One can almost chart Burns's journey by the poems he wrote and the folk songs he picked up and re-worked, like this one from the Moray Firth:

> A' the lads o' Thornie-bank
>   When they gae to the shore o' Bucky,
> They'll step in and tak a pint
>   Wi' Lady Onlie, honest lucky.

> Lady Onlie, honest lucky,
> Brews gude ale at shore o' Bucky;
> I wish her sale for her gude ale,
> The best on a' the shore o' Bucky.

He loved genuinely local songs reflecting the habits and traditions and work patterns of a region:

GREAT BRITONS

Up wi' the carls of Dysart,
And the lads o' Buckhiven,
And the Kimmers o' Largo,
And the lasses o' Leven.
Hey ca' thro' ca' thro'
For we hae mickle a do,
Hey ca' thro' ca' thro'
For we hae mickle a do.

This is a fisher song from Fife. Did Burns just collect it, or re-make it from a surviving chorus, or perhaps add a final stanza?

Not great poetry, these casual little folk songs or songs in the folk idiom. But they reveal one of the sources of Burns's strength – his relish for the rhythms of life and labour among ordinary people. Landscape for him was always a landscape with figures. He did not romanticise mountains or sea (he never mentions the mountains of Arran, visible from the Ayrshire coast). Nature is the environment in which rural labour takes place. The 'burnie' 'trots' or 'toddles' down the hill. By its banks on a summer evening the farmer walks with his girl, or lies with her in the grass.

O kissin is the key o' luve,
An clappin is the lock,
An makin-of's the best thing,
That e'er a young Thing got.

On his Highland tour Burns was entertained by the Duke of Atholl at Blair Atholl, and would have stayed longer than the two days he did stay (as he was pressed to do) if his fellow traveller William Nicol had not got jealous and pulled him away. Nicol was jealous again when Burns was invited by the Duke and Duchess of Gordon to stay at Gordon Castle, Fochabers, while Nicol himself had to stay at the local inn. He insisted on their leaving, which was a great pity, for the next day the powerful Henry Dundas, later Viscount Melville, was coming to stay at Gordon Castle and could have helped Burns to get the Excise job he was still vainly seeking.

Burns was back in Edinburgh on 16 September 1787, but on 4 October he was off on his travels again, this time with Dr James Adair, son of an Ayr doctor, whom Burns had met through the Reverend George Lawrie. He visited Stirling (for the second time) and then went on to Harvieston, Clackmannanshire, where they stayed with a gentleman farmer called Chalmers whose wife was related to Gavin Hamilton. Burns fell in love with the daughter, Peggy Chalmers, and wanted to marry her. But, though she appears to have been fond of him, she was not prepared to risk marriage with an impecunious rural poet. Peggy Chalmers was the most intelligent and best educated of all the girls Burns fell in love with. If he

Peggy Chalmers as painted by John Irvine c.1800

had married her, some of the social tensions with which he lived all his life may have been resolved. When he finally married Jean Armour, none of Burns's friends considered her fit for genteel company, nor did she, for she knew nothing of the fashionable or intellectual world. So when he accepted invitations to the houses of ladies and gentlemen he left his wife behind. She did not complain.

He kept on falling in love with other girls, but he couldn't get Jean out of his system, even when he was having the most strange love affair of his life, with the pretty Edinburgh grass-widow Agnes M'Lehose. He met her in Edinburgh in December 1787, when he was there again. She was living separate from her dissolute husband in a flat in Potter Row, that fine old Edinburgh street that I used to walk along every day on my way to Edinburgh University. It has since been pulled down by the vandals who have destroyed all that area around George Square, Edinburgh's first 'New Town', done in a native, vernacular classical style, unlike the more elegant and international New Town to the north. Burns had hurt his leg and was unable to call on her as he had promised, so they began a correspondence which became progressively warmer. He called himself Sylvander and her Clarinda and developed a curious hot-house love affair in a high neo-classic style. Then, when his leg was better, he paid her visits. We don't know exactly what went on in that flat in Potter Row. We know what Burns wanted, and that Clarinda, who made much of her religious sentiments, resisted his physical advances. Certainly Burns worked himself into a state of great physical excitement, but seems to have relieved it eventually with girls of the town. It was Clarinda's discovery of this, together with Burns's eventual recognition of Jean as his wife (as under Scots law he could do, retroactively) that caused the break between them, marked by the last of Burns's poems to her, the only one where he struck the note of true passion:

> *Had we never lov'd sae kindly,*
> *Had we never lov'd sae blindly!*
> *Never met – or never parted,*
> *We had ne'er been broken-hearted.*

All his other poems to Clarinda were written in standard English.

Burns to James Smith, 28 April, 1788:

... to let you into the secrets of my pericranium, there is, you must know, a certain clean-limbed, handsome, bewitching young hussy of your acquaintance, to whom I have lately and privately given matrimonial title to my corpus ... I hate to presage ill-luck; and as my girl has been *doubly* kinder to me than even the best of women usually are to their partners of our sex, in similar circumstances, I reckon on twelve times a brace of children against I celebrate my twelfth wedding-day.

So he was now married to Jean, long-suffering, loving Jean, who tolerated his extra-marital adventures ('Oor Rab should hae had twa wives', she once said) and even brought up one of his illegitimate children with her own. She had no part in his intellectual or high social life. But she could sing his songs, and for all his wanderings he loved her.

In June 1788 Burns finally decided to accept Patrick Miller's offer of a farm in Dumfriesshire, and he moved there that month. Ellisland it was called, six and a half miles north-west of Dumfries on the west bank of the river Nith. It had no farmhouse, and he left his family at Mauchline while

An anonymous watercolour of Agnes M'Lehose (Clarinda)

one was being built. Jean joined him in December, to look after the dairy.

Burns was always unlucky with his farms, and Ellisland was no exception. In September 1810 Patrick Miller admitted that the farm he had leased to Burns was a ruinous bargain:

When I purchased this estate about twenty-five years ago, I had not seen it. *It was in the most miserable state of exhaustion*, and all the tenants in poverty . . . *When I went to view my purchase, I was so much disgusted for eight or ten days, that I then meant never to return to this country.*

Burns did his best, but by the spring of 1790 he knew that he could never farm Ellisland profitably. Fortunately, he was now at last successful in getting an Excise appointment, in charge of the 'Dumfries first Itinerary' at a salary of fifty pounds a year. He had to ride around the countryside checking weights and measures and watching for smuggling.

On 11 November 1791, having signed a formal renunciation of the Ellisland lease, Burns moved with his family to Dumfries, and lived there till his death on 21 July 1796. At first he rented a second-floor flat in what is now Bank Street from Captain John Hamilton, then, in the spring of 1793, he moved to a larger house in Mill Street. The house in Mill Street he rented from the same Captain John Hamilton for £8 per annum. It is now a Burns museum. His 'local', as we would say, in Dumfries was the Globe Inn at 56 High Street. There he made love to the landlady's niece, Anna Park, who helped at the bar, and wrote for her the song 'Yestreen I had a pint o'wine'. It was Anna's daughter by Burns that Jean cheerfully brought up with her own.

Burns made new friends in Dumfries. There was the radical doctor, William Maxwell, ardent supporter of the French Revolution. There was John Syme, convivial son of a Kirkudbrightshire laird, who frequently entertained Burns at his villa, Ryedale, on the west side of the Nith. Syme and Burns toured Galloway together in the summer of 1794. There was Alexander Findlater, Excise Supervisor at Dumfries and therefore Burns's boss. There was John Lewars, a fellow exciseman, whose sister Jessie helped to nurse Burns in his last illness and to whom the dying poet wrote one of his tenderest songs to a favourite air of hers that she had played to him on her piano:

> Oh wert thou in the cauld blast,
>   On yonder lea, on yonder lea;
> My plaidie to the angry airt,   [airt = direction]
>   I'd shelter thee, I'd shelter thee:
> Or did misfortune's bitter storms
>   Around thee blaw, around thee blaw,
> Thy bield should be my bosom,   [bield = shelter]
>   To share it a', to share it a'.

The Globe Inn, Dumfries, frequented by Burns

It was a strange and moving reversal of roles, for it was the mortally sick poet who needed protection: sturdy Jessie was well able to look after herself. (She later married a Dumfries solicitor and had seven children.)

Another friend was the Dumfries school teacher James Gray, who after Burns's death defended him from the charge of habitual drunkenness:

It came under my own view professionally, that he superintended the education of his children with a degree of care that I have never seen surpassed by any parent in any rank of life whatever. In the bosom of his family he spent many a delightful hour in directing the studies of his eldest son, a boy of uncommon talents. I have frequently found him explaining to this youth, then not more than nine years of age, the English poets, from Shakespeare to Gray, or storing his mind with examples of heroic virtue, as they live in the pages of our more celebrated historians. I would ask any person of common candour, if employments like these are consistent with habitual drunkenness.

It was a hard drinking age. Burns's problem was that when he attended the parties of the gentry, as he continued to be invited to do, he was not expected to behave with the freedom used by other heavy drinking guests, who were landowners and not peasant poets. An incident that occurred at the end of December clearly illustrates the uncertainties and dangers of Burns's social position.

While he was at Ellisland Burns made a friend of a retired army captain named Robert Riddell, who lived on the Glenriddell estate at Friar's Carse, less than a mile north of Ellisland. Riddell was an amateur antiquary interested in Scottish songs; he actually composed some song tunes for which Burns wrote words. Burns was allowed to go freely to the Hermitage on the Glenriddell estate, and he used to meditate and write poetry there. Robert Riddell had a younger brother Walter, whom Burns also became friendly with. He became particularly friendly with Walter's vivacious and attractive wife, Maria, and exchanged lively letters with her.

One day in late December 1793, when Maria Riddell's husband was away in the West Indies, there was a party at Friar's Carse to which Burns was invited. It is not quite clear exactly what happened, but it seems that, after some heavy drinking, the men in the party decided to act out the 'Rape of the Sabine Women'. Burns was egged on to act out his part with some vigour, perhaps on Maria, but possibly on Robert Riddell's wife Elizabeth. We do not know exactly what he did, but it certainly gave great offence to the whole Riddell family. What hurt and angered Burns most was that Maria proceeded to ostracise him. Furious and humiliated, Burns turned from affection and admiration to bitter anger, and wrote some very nasty verse lampoons about Maria. They were reconciled in the end, but only when Burns was literally a dying man.

This incident shows clearly the precariousness of Burns's social position. His social superiors could get drunk and make fools of themselves at parties as a matter of course; but Burns had to watch his step. And of course when he went to these parties he left Jean at home. She belonged to a different world. Burns lived simultaneously in these two divided and distinguished worlds, which represented a divided Scotland – the English-oriented Scotland and the genteel tradition of the *literati* on the one hand, and the native traditions of the Scottish countryside on the other.

If Burns had to watch his step socially it was even more important for him to be careful politically. All his life he was a passionate egalitarian, and when the French Revolution broke out in 1789 he hailed it as the dawn of freedom. But as an Excise officer he was a government servant. In 1790 he was promoted to the Dumfries '3d, or Tobacco, Division', with his salary increased to £75 a year. In 1792 he actually led a boarding party on to a grounded schooner engaged in smuggling on the Solway Firth.

But indications of his revolutionary sympathies brought him into trouble with the authorities. An official inquiry into Burns's loyalty took place in December 1792. When he heard that this was about to happen, he was in his own words 'confounded and distracted'. He would lose his job – his family would starve. He was in a panic. He wrote to his friend and patron Robert Graham of Fintry, a member of the Board of Excise:

Sir, you are a Husband – and a father – you know what you would feel, to see the much-loved wife of your bosom, and your helpless, prattling little ones, turned adrift into the world, degraded and disgraced, from a situation in which they had been respectable and respected, and left almost without the necessary support of a miserable existence. Alas, Sir! must I think that such, soon will be my lot!

The matter blew over at last. One of the Excise supervisors, William Corbet, came down from Glasgow to conduct the investigation, and Alexander Findlater, the Dumfries supervisor, testified that Burns was 'exact, vigilant, and sober; that, in fact, he was one of the best officers in the district'. He was found guiltless of any disloyalty. But he had had a shock he was never to forget.

He had in fact been very reckless in both public and private utterances and in spite of his shock he could still be. His old friend Mrs Dunlop broke with him when in a letter to her as late as January 1795 he referred to Louis XVI and Marie Antoinette, who had been executed in 1793, as 'a perjured Blockhead and an unprincipled prostitute'. Two of Mrs Dunlop's daughters had married French royalist refugees. She was bitterly offended, and would not reply to his hurt letters asking what he had done wrong. Only when she knew that he was dying did she relent, and one of the very last things he read was a friendly message from her.

Publicly, Burns took the line that he became disillusioned with France 'when she came to show her old avidity for conquest, in annexing Savoy, &c. to her dominions and invading the rights of Holland' – as he wrote to Graham of Fintry. And when Britain declared war on France he supported the British Government. When there was the threat of a French invasion in the spring of 1795 Burns helped to organise the Dumfries company of volunteers and wrote a song:

> *Does haughty Gaul invasion threat,*
> *Then let the louns beware, Sir,*
> *There's wooden Walls upon our seas,*
> *And volunteers on shore, Sir: . . .*

All this time he was continuing to collect, improve, rewrite and create Scottish songs for Johnson and Thomson. Thomson was a more genteel person than Johnson, and often pressed Burns to make his poems more English and more suitable to what he considered high-class taste. On 16 September 1792 he wrote to Thomson:

As the request you make to me will positively add to my enjoyment in complying with it, I shall enter into your undertaking with all the small portion of abilities I have, sustained to their utmost by the impulse of Enthusiasm . . . if you are for *English* verses, there is, on my part, an end of the matter. Whether in the simplicity of the Ballad or the pathos of the Song, I can only hope to please myself in being allowed at least a sprinkling of our native tongue.

He went on:

As to any remuneration, you may think my Songs either *above*, or *below* price; for they shall absolutely be the one or the other. In the honest enthusiasm with which I embark on your undertaking, to talk of money, wages, fee, hire, &c., would be downright Sodomy of Soul.

Again, on 26 October 1792:

Let me tell you, that you are too fastidious in your ideas of Songs and ballads . . . let me remark to you, in the sentiment and style of our Scottish airs, there is a pastoral simplicity, a something that one may call, the Doric style and dialect of vocal music, to which a dash of our native tongue and manners is particularly, nay peculiarly apposite.

The letters Burns wrote to Thomson and Johnson show him both the eager enthusiast and the conscientious craftsman. He was an absolute genius in framing words to fit an existing tune and often goes into considerable technical detail in discussing questions of phrasing.

The volumes of Johnson's *Scots Musical Museum* and Thomson's *Select Scottish Airs* contain an extraordinary range of songs contributed, mended, restored or wholly composed by Burns. There is the hauntingly beautiful 'Ca' the Yowes to the Knowes' which he first heard sung by 'a worthy little fellow of a Clergyman, a Mr Clunzie, who sung it charmingly; and at my request, Mr Clarke took it down from his singing'. (Stephen Clarke was the Edinburgh musician who helped Burns in transcribing and arranging melodies.) Though Burns was enchanted with the tune he was not satisfied with the words sung by Mr Clunzie, even after he had adapted them, and he produced another version, where the sense of hush and benediction is beautifully rendered.

There is the charmingly lilting and cunningly constructed song he wrote to one of Jean's favourite airs:

> *O luve will venture in where it daur na weel be seen,*
> *O luve will venture in where wisdom ance has been;*
> *But I will down yon river rove, amang the woods sae green,*
> *And a' to pu' a posie to my ain dear May.*

There is 'A Red, Red, Rose', which he claims simply to have picked up but which I believe certainly bears marks of his own work. It is the perfect rendering of that combination of swagger and tender protectiveness that characterises the male in love:

> *As fair art thou, my bonie lass,*
> *So deep in luve am I;*
> *And I will luve thee still, my Dear,*
> *Till a' the seas gang dry . . .*

There is the jauntingly lilting 'O Whistle, and I'll come to ye, my Lad', again a reworking of an old theme. There is the simply moving 'O lay thy Loof [hand] in mine, Lass', which like so many of Burns's songs must be sung to be appreciated, for it is written to be emotionally filled out by the tune. There is one of the finest drinking songs in the world, 'O Willie brewed a Peck of Maut', with its splendid chorus:

> *We are na fou, we're nae that fou,*
> *But just a drappie in our e'e;*
> *The cock may craw, the day may daw,*
> *And ay we'll taste the barley bree.*

There is the mixture of love, sadness and ritual, in his famous poem of lovers' parting:

> *Go fetch to me a pint o' wine,*
> *And fill it in a silver tassie;*
> *That I may drink, before I go,*
> *A service to my bonie lassie . . .*

135

There is the fiercely democratic 'A Man's a Man for a' that' and the equally passionately patriotic 'Scots wha hae'. There are work songs, comic songs, narrative songs, satirical songs – songs in almost every mood and style. He continued working on songs almost up to the very day of his death, 21 July 1796.

He was writing other poetry too, of course, as well as carrying on his continuous and arduous Excise duties. The most remarkable poem he wrote after his Edinburgh visits was 'Tam o' Shanter'. He wrote this in 1790 for Captain Grose, the antiquary, who wanted a poem based on a local legend to illustrate a picture of Alloway Kirk in his *Antiquities of Scotland*. It is Burns's only sustained narrative poem, and shows what he could do in this form when he set his mind to it.

The poem opens by setting an indoor scene: a cosy pub interior on market day, where the farmers are gathered to drink after the day's bargaining, before going home. They all disperse, except Tam himself, and Souter Johnny. Tam can't bring himself to leave the warm fire and the cheerful landlady to go back to his own sullen wife. After the incisively etched interior, with the verse moving at various speeds to indicate the change between humorous, ironic and mock-moral moods, we are taken outside, and Tam's adventure with the witches of Alloway Kirk. He gets home in the end, but just.

Early in 1796 it was clear that Burns was very ill. He writes to Johnson on 24 February:

Mr Clarke will have acquainted you with the unfortunate reasons for my long silence. When I get a little more health, you shall hear from me at large on the subject of the songs.

To Thomson in April of the same year he wrote:

Almost ever since I wrote you last, I have only known Existence by the pressure of the heavy hand of Sickness; and have counted time by the repercussions of Pain! Rheumatism, Cold, and Fever have formed, to me, a terrible Trinity in Unity, which makes me close my eyes in misery, and open them without hope.

On 3 July his doctor sent him to Brow, on the Solway Firth, on the grounds that sea-bathing would be good for his condition. Not surprisingly, it did not help. Jean was expecting another baby, and he wrote to her father asking him to send Mrs Armour to help her. On 12 July he wrote in anguish to Thomson:

After all my boasted independence, curst necessity compels me to implore you for five pounds. – A cruel scoundrel of a Haberdasher to whom I owe an account, taking it into his head that I am dying, has commenced a process, and will infallibly put me into jail. Do, for God's sake, send me that sum, and that by return of post. Forgive me this earnestness, but the horrors of a jail have made me half distracted.

– I do not ask all this gratuitously; for upon returning health, I hereby promise and engage to furnish you with five pounds' worth of the neatest song-genius you have seen. – I tryed my hand on Rothiemurche this morning . . .

'I tried my hand on Rothiemurche this morning.' Rothiemurche was a traditional song tune to which Burns was writing new words. Yet he was a dying man, and in desperate mental anguish at the thought of being prosecuted and jailed for debt.

He returned to Dumfries on 18 July, to find Jean expecting her baby imminently. He wrote desperately to his father-in-law. It was his last letter:

My dear Sir,

Do, for Heaven's sake, Send Mrs Armour here immediately. My wife is hourly expecting to be put to bed. Good God! What a situation for her to be in, poor girl, without a friend! . . .

Three days later he died in the Mill Street house. His friend John Syme arranged a military funeral, with a procession moving from Dumfries Town Hall over a mile and a half to the cemetery. The streets were lined by troops from the Angus Fencibles and the Cinque Ports Cavalry, both then stationed in Dumfries. Burns after all had been prominent in organising the Dumfriesshire Volunteers. A firing party of fellow volunteers marched at the head of the procession, and behind them the band of the Cinque Ports Cavalry played the Dead March from *Saul*. Back at the house in Mill Street Jean gave birth to a boy as the funeral was taking place.

Burns did not die of drink, as legend long maintained. He liked his dram like most Scotsmen, and the social tensions under which he lived sometimes drove him to excess. But at least one medical authority has given it as his opinion that Burns's life might well have been shorter if he had never taken spirits. He died of rheumatic fever, and modern medical opinion also diagnoses that bacterial endocarditis may well have been present terminally. Today his symptoms would have been recognised much earlier, and he would have been treated with antibiotics and perhaps also with cortisone.

He was reconciled with Maria Riddell shortly before his death. When he was at Brow she was staying nearby, and invited him to dinner. She sent her carriage to fetch him. She described what happened:

I was struck with his appearance on entering the room. The stamp of death was impressed on his features. He seemed already touching the brink of eternity. His first salutation was 'Well, Madam, have you any commands for the other world?' At table he ate little or nothing, and he complained of having lost entirely the tone of his stomach . . . He spoke of his death without any of the ostentation of philosophy, but with firmness as well as feeling.

He talked about his children, and was especially proud of the 'promising genius' of his eldest son. He then went on to talk of his literary fame:

He said that he was well aware that his death would occasion some noise, and that every scrap of his writing would be revived against him to the injury of his future reputation: that letters and verses written with unguarded and improper free-dom, and which he earnestly wished to have buried in oblivion, would be handed about by idle vanity or malevolence, when no dread of his resentment would restrain them, or prevent the censures of shrill-tongued malice, or the insidious sarcasms of envy, from pouring forth all their venom to blast his fame.

It didn't happen like that. Though nineteenth-century editors and biographers destroyed some of his writing they considered improper and hushed up others, today we even have a paperback edition of *The Merry Muses*, the collection of bawdy songs Burns made – some written by himself – for his friends in the Crochallan Fencibles. He could not have imagined the love and celebratory enthusiasm with which he would be remembered. Nor did he know that the song 'Auld Lang Syne', which he sent to Thomson as an old song he had discovered and which appeared in the 1796 volume of Johnson's *Scots Musical Museum* as well as in the 1799 volume of Thomson's *Select Scottish Airs*, would take its place throughout the world as the great song of parting. He sent various versions to various correspondents, and there is no doubt that although the song itself is very old and the chorus in Burns's song is an old chorus, the words as we have them are largely Burns's own. The note of remembered friendship he introduces so simply and poignantly in the second and third stanzas could only have come from him:

> *We twa hae run about the braes,*
> *And pu'd the gowans fine;*
> *But we've wandered money a weary foot,*
> *Sin auld lang syne.*

> *We twa hae paidl'd i' the burn,*
> *Frae morning sun till dine;*
> *But seas between us braid hae roar'd*
> *Sin auld lang syne.*

> *For auld lang syne, &c.*

How many summer days in my own childhood have my brother and I spent 'paidling in the burn frae morning sun till dine'. When during the war we were separated by two oceans, these words kept haunting me. That is what Burns does to one.

The house in Mill Street where Burns died on 21 July 1796

MARLBOROUGH

CORRELLI BARNETT

Had it not been for John Churchill, First Duke of Marlborough, the world might today be speaking French instead of English. Britain herself might have remained just what she was in Marlborough's youth – a second-rank power, an off-shore island; in fact, almost a French satellite. And without him, English ideals of individual freedom and parliamentary government might never have been exported across the globe. For when he first took the field as Queen Anne's Captain-General, the France of Louis XIV, a royal tyranny, was the super-power of the age, threatening permanently to dominate Europe and its colonies. And residing in France under Louis's protection was the Roman Catholic pretender to the thrones of England and Scotland, the so-called 'James III', son of the exiled James II. The British kingdoms therefore lay in future danger of being ruled by a monarch determined to impose Roman Catholicism as the national religion, to extinguish the burgeoning powers of Parliament, and to turn Britain once again into a virtual satellite of France. All these dangers were averted by Marlborough's leadership in war – and another, more splendid, future opened for the English-speaking peoples.

However, the fascination of Marlborough's story lies not only in his achievement, but also in his own character and personality. Some famous historians have portrayed him as a kind of remote diplomatic and military machine; nothing more than the public figure to be seen in the grandiose portraits of the time. Yet his own letters reveal a very different individual – intensely human and vulnerable, a man with a streak of weakness, often under great stress and beset by anxieties. The dignified, calm outward manner was achieved only at the cost of tremendous self-control. And behind his apparent assurance there lay a profound sense of insecurity. All this renders him in many ways a much more interesting figure than our other great military hero, Wellington.

Yet the Duke of Marlborough was much more than just a soldier; he was a great international statesman also. No other British general in history, not even Wellington, had to endure the same degree of strain or carry the same weight and variety of responsibility.

John Churchill was born at Ashe House, near Axminster in Somerset, on 26 May 1650, in an England deeply divided between royalists and parliamentarians – 'Roundhead and Cavalier'. In January of the previous year Charles I had been beheaded in Whitehall; England had become a republican Commonwealth under Oliver Cromwell. John Churchill's own family circumstances were typical of the deep rift through English society caused by the Civil War. His father, Winston Churchill, a Cavalier of modest fortune, had been dispossessed and fined by the new regime for backing the King. So Winston and his wife were taken in by his widowed mother-in law, Lady Drake, the owner of Ashe House. But she was a parliamentary supporter, and Ashe had been partly burned during the Civil War by royalist troops. Lady Drake was too poor even to repair the damaged roof for some years.

Jack Churchill therefore grew up in relative poverty, without his own home, amid all the family bitterness and division which mirrored a divided country. In this grim and insecure childhood lay one of the key influences on his character and future conduct.

The restoration of Charles II in 1660, two years after Cromwell's death, gave hope to old Cavaliers like Winston Churchill that they would at last come into their own. But since King Charles himself was short of cash, he had to give them and their families honours and jobs at court instead of compensating them financially for their losses. In 1663 Jack's father, now Sir Winston, became Junior Clerk Comptroller of the King's Household. Nevertheless he died heavily in debt – partly because he was always in a muddle over money. So Jack learned two great lessons from his boyhood: avoid being caught on the wrong side, and count the pennies.

When Jack was fifteen King Charles appointed him page to his brother, James, Duke of York, the heir to the throne and a devout Roman Catholic, by way of a further act of kindness to the Churchill family. Jack's elder sister, Arabella, had already become James's mistress. A poor boy himself, Jack now lived among the beautiful and the great in the bawdy, gaudy court in the old palace of Whitehall. He learned what it was to depend on patronage; he learned the deference of the servant; he learned to charm. In fact, by the time he was twenty he had come to be reckoned among the most handsome and accomplished of the young rakes about court. In 1673 he even added the King's own mistress, Barbara Castlemaine, to his game bag. Their affair lasted some three years, and her last child, a daughter, was almost certainly his. That he should have satisfied so passionate a woman as Barbara Castlemaine belies that later image of Marlborough, created by historians and painters, of a cold, calm figure devoid of fire or dash. Indeed, on one occasion Jack found himself caught in Barbara's bedroom by the arrival of the King. Quick-thinking, quick-acting, he jumped out of the first-floor window and escaped. Barbara was said to have given him £500 as a reward, which Jack, shrewd and careful with money, used to buy an annuity, the foundation of his ultimately vast fortune.

By now he was already a soldier with a rising reputation for gallantry and leadership. In 1667, at the age of seventeen, he had been commissioned as an ensign in the First Guards (now the Grenadier Guards), thanks to the influence of his patron, the Duke of York. So the story goes, young Jack fell under the spell of pipe and drum, gold and scarlet, one day when he watched the King's Guards at exercise in St James's Park, and

John Churchill as a very young man; miniature by an unknown artist

there and then decided to become a soldier. A year later he found himself on active service in Tangier, which had come to the English crown as part of the dowry of Charles II's Portuguese wife. There, skirmishing with the Moors in the heat and dust of Moroccan summers, he first learned his trade – as good a training as later English subalterns enjoyed on the north-west frontier of India fighting the Afghans and Pathans. He also saw service on shipboard with the English squadron in the Mediterranean, and in 1672 was with his patron the Duke of York (then the Lord High Admiral of England) in the fierce battle of Sole Bay, off the Suffolk coast, against the Dutch. Here was another element in the future allied commander – an understanding of sea-warfare in the age of sail, and of the limitations imposed by the vagaries of wind and tide. He was never to make the mistakes of such land-lubbers as Napoleon or Hitler when they sought to conduct maritime strategy.

But in peacetime the English forces offered little hope of advancement for an ambitious officer; they amounted to hardly more than the royal guards, a handful of newly raised regiments, and fortress garrisons. And, unlike European states, England was rarely at war, and then only for brief periods. Instead English and Scots soldiers went off to serve in the 'foreign legions' of other armies, such as the Dutch or the French.

In the 1670s the French army served as the model for Europe. It had been re-organised by brilliant war ministers; it was led by such outstanding commanders as Turenne, and Louis XIV employed it in campaign after campaign aimed at expanding France at the expense of her neighbours. Charles II connived at this process; even on one occasion became France's ally. For Charles II needed Louis's secret subsidies in order to remain independent of parliament. England's role in the European power struggle was one of impotence, if not even that of a French satellite.

In 1674-5 John Churchill served with Louis XIV's royal English Regiment in the Low Countries and southern Germany, learning the art of war with the finest army of the age. At the siege of Maastricht he and his English soldiers were the first to plant the fleur-de-lys standard of France on the breached ramparts. The great Turenne himself praised Churchill – 'my handsome Englishman' – in dispatches for his bravery and energetic leadership at the battle of Enzheim. Churchill even met Louis XIV himself, the so-called 'Sun King', on being promoted. All this was priceless experience for the future, for he came to know at first hand the French army and the commanders he was later to fight.

But in 1675 he turned down an offer of promotion to Lieutenant-Colonel of the Royal English Regiment. The French ambassador in London reported why to the Minister of War in Paris: 'Churchill has preferred to serve Sarah Jennings, who is very pretty, than to be Lieutenant-colonel . . . '

Sarah Jennings was only fifteen when Jack Churchill met her at Court that year, a Maid of Honour to the Duchess of York. Behind the painter's conventions of the period the first known portrait of her shows a sharp-eyed, intelligent, strong-willed young woman. She came from the same kind of background as John Churchill himself – minor gentlefolk with little money. Her widowed mother, a shrewish and embittered woman, lived in rooms at Court, and she and her teenaged daughter quarrelled ferociously.

For the first and last time John Churchill really fell in love. But he did not find it an easy courtship. There were family complications, for his parents wished him to marry a suitable but ugly heiress. He had to disentangle himself from Barbara Castlemaine. And Sarah herself, though she fell deeply in love with him too, was shrewd and self-controlled enough not to commit herself to this notorious rake until she was really sure of him. She had no wish to become just another Maid of Honour with child. So for two years she kept him floundering on the hook of his love for her.

Painting of Sarah Jennings aged 15; attributed to Simon Verelst,
it hung in Sarah's dressing-room at Holywell House

The hasty notes which he wrote her amid all the bustle of court life and their duties as members of the Yorks' household have survived. They tell the story of his courting; bear witness just how deeply he wanted her.

I fancy by this time you are awake, which makes me now send to know how you are . . .

. . . pray let me hear from you, and I beg that I may be blessed this night in being with you . . .

. . . I was last night at the ball, in hopes to have seen what I love above my own soul, but I was not so happy, for I could see you nowhere . . .

. . . I beg that I may then have leave to see you tonight at eight, for believe me, my love persuades me that it is an age since I was with you . . .

During the winter of 1677-8 they were secretly married. Henceforward they were to form a partnership against the world. But of all the letters Sarah must have written him during their married life, only one short note dating from around 1690 has survived, for Sarah insisted that they be destroyed. Yet this one note is enough to reveal the fierceness of her love and loyalty:

Wherever you are, whilst I have life, my soul shall follow you, my ever dear Lord Marl; and wherever I am I should only kill the time, wish for night that I may sleep and hope the next day to hear from you.

They began life together in rooms in the rambling old Palace of Whitehall, of which nothing now remains but the Banqueting House. Soon Sarah and the Duke of York's younger daughter, Princess Anne, became the most intimate of friends. Anne, a plain and timid girl five years younger than Sarah, had an almost schoolgirl crush on her brilliant, beautiful and masterful friend. When Anne married Prince George of Denmark in 1683, she appointed Sarah to be the Lady of the Bedchamber in her new household. In the closeness of domestic life, their friendship thickened even further. They shared the experience of almost annual pregnancies and the horrors of seventeenth-century childbirth, and the grief at the early death from disease of the children so painfully produced. Because Anne wanted no barriers of rank to stand between them, they began to call each other 'Mrs Morley' and 'Mrs Freeman' – and Sarah's husband became 'Mr Freeman', Anne's trusted protector and advisor. It was unique, this intimacy between subjects and royalty, and became John and Sarah's strongest asset as they patiently set out to raise themselves from poverty and obscurity to high position and a great fortune.

In 1685 John's patron the Duke of York succeeded to the throne as James II, and John himself became Baron Churchill of Sandridge. That summer Churchill took the field for the first time in eleven years – against the Protestant rebel, the Duke of Monmouth, and his army of West Country peasants. As brigadier and second-in-command of the royal army, he relentlessly hounded the Duke of Monmouth back to Weston Zoyland, near Bridgwater. In the night hours of the morning of 6 July 1685 the now desperate Monmouth advanced to attack the royal army at Sedgemoor. He was defeated and his forces scattered – thanks largely to Churchill's personal leadership in the battle, culminating in a charge at the head of the Royal Dragoons, of which he was himself the colonel. The Sedgemoor campaign shows Churchill at a turning-point in his development as a commander – strategic grasp, immense energy, a finger-tip feel for the run of a battle.

Queen Anne as a girl; engraved by R. Thompson after Lely

Now the future seemed bright with promise for John and Sarah. But instead the next ten years proved turbulent enough, with times of heavy setback and disappointment.

James II was a fervent Catholic. He was also resolved to turn England into an absolute monarchy on the model of Louis XIV's France. As a result his overwhelmingly Protestant subjects came year by year increasingly to fear that both their Religion and their parliamentary constitution were in peril. So a group of great noblemen secretly invited William of Orange, the Protestant Dutch leader married to James's elder daughter Mary, to bring an army to England and eject James from the throne. In 1688 England was facing the prospect of another civil war – fuelled by just such a deadly blend of politics and religious feeling as can still be seen in Northern Ireland today.

John Churchill now had some hard choices to make. He himself was a Protestant; so too were Sarah and Princess Anne. But he was also one of King James's closest and most trusted associates. He had therefore to balance his religion, the best interests of his country, and – be it said – his own interest, against his obligations of personal loyalty to James.

What did he do? He marched out with James as second-in-command of the royal army to meet William of Orange's forces which had landed at Torbay. On the night of 4 December 1688, he left the royal camp at Salisbury and rode over to join William. Meanwhile, by a pre-arranged plan, Princess Anne had been spirited out of London under Sarah's care to Protestant supporters in the North of England.

James II's nerve was shattered by such desertions, and, ordering his army to be disbanded, he fled the country. William became king – and, thanks in great degree to John Churchill, without a shooting war. Now here were all the hallmarks of Churchill's later generalship – secrecy, deception, last-minute surprise, decisive action at the key moment. But what of the morality of it? Some historians have accused him of 'betraying' James; of being just a careerist who switched to the winning side. There is no doubt that he *was* a careerist – if that is a bad thing. But he might have served his career just as well by staying with James and defeating William of Orange's army. As for being personally disloyal to James he surely owed a higher loyalty to the good of his country, just like the German generals in regard to Hitler during the Second World War. No one applauds the 'loyalty' of those generals who did choose to serve Hitler to the end. Next year the new king made John Churchill Earl of Marlborough.

Now England and Scotland (not yet united into one kingdom) found themselves at last drawn into the thick of the struggle to halt the expansion of French power. For William of Orange's own main purpose in accepting the thrones of the British kingdoms was to add their weight to his alliance of smaller European states against Louis XIV.

In 1689 the exiled James II sought to conquer Ireland with an army of French troops and Catholic Irishmen, as a springboard for recovering his crown. But he was defeated at the Battle of the Boyne by William, who for this reason remains to this day a hero to Protestant Ulstermen. Meanwhile Marlborough was commanding the English contingent in the allied army in Flanders. He saved the day at the battle of Walcourt by his swift tactical grasp and a personal charge at the head of the Life Guards. The allied C-in-C reported to William: 'The Earl of Marlborough is assuredly one of the bravest men I know. In spite of his youth he has displayed in this one battle greater military capacity than do most generals after a long series of wars.'

Next year Marlborough, charged by the king with defence of England in the face of a French invasion threat, helped William's final victory in Ireland by capturing the French supply ports of Cork and Kinsale in brilliantly executed combined operations. 'No officer living who has seen so little service as my Lord Marlborough,' wrote William, 'is so fit for great commands.'

But instead of 'great commands' Marlborough found himself in 1692 a prisoner in the Tower of London – a few months after the King had dismissed both the Marlboroughs from all their court offices. It marked the nadir of their high ambitions. In fact Marlborough's imprisonment lasted only six weeks. He and other notables had been framed by a clumsy plot to incriminate them in treasonable dealings with the exiled James II. But although this plot was soon exposed, Marlborough *had* been in touch with James II's agents. Some historians have alleged from Jacobite documents that he had even passed on military secrets. However, comparison of dates shows that he was careful only to pass on information already public knowledge – too late to be useful to the French.

Here was another Marlborough – secretive, cunning, determined to be a survivor in an age of revolution and plot, 're-insuring' with James just in case the wheel of fortune should ever bring James back to the throne. Yet William had dismissed the Marlboroughs for a different reason altogether. Marlborough had made all too public his resentment at the King's preference for fellow Dutchmen in high places. Ill-feeling between the two men was worsened by a sisterly quarrel between Queen Mary and Princess Anne, Sarah's dear friend Mrs Morley. William came to see Marlborough as a dangerous focus of court opposition, and finally made up his mind to sack him. Here was another lesson that Marlborough was never to forget: that plain speaking and an open stand, could lead to

John Churchill; by or after Kneller

loss of office and a plunge back into insecurity and financial worry.

After 1697 Europe lay at peace. But Louis XIV's territorial ambitions were only sleeping. In 1701 he allowed his grandson Philip of Anjou to become King Philip IV of Spain, in plain breach of a treaty with William of Orange. As much of the territory of modern Belgium then belonged to the Spanish throne, this raised the menace of Bourbon rule from Cadiz to Brussels, perhaps one day under a single king. Control of the Spanish Empire in Central and South America and the East would enable Louis XIV to dominate world trade. So William set about creating a fresh alliance to prevent this link between the French and Spanish crowns, and place a son of the Habsburg Emperor on the Spanish throne instead, as Charles III.

But William knew that his health was failing, and that someone else would have to lead this coalition in war. That someone must be English, because England would provide the mainstay of the alliance; must be an able soldier; must be an accomplished diplomat as well. And William also saw that this someone must be a man who would enjoy the full confidence of his own successor, Princess Anne. Only Marlborough fitted the bill. In 1701 William gave him the task of negotiating the new alliance. Marlborough accomplished it with outstanding charm and diplomatic skill. In Lord Chesterfield's words, he 'possessed the graces in the highest degree . . . His figure was beautiful, but his manner was irresistible, by either man or woman.'

On 20 February 1702 the Marlboroughs' dearest friend Mrs Morley became Queen Anne of England and Scotland. And the Marlboroughs – Mr and Mrs Freeman – had become the most powerful figures in the realm; Marlborough himself the Queen's Captain-General and England's war leader. In May war was declared on France and Marlborough sailed to the Netherlands to take up command of the allied army. He was 52. Like his illustrious descendant Winston Churchill in 1930, he had been swept from retirement and apparent failure to the top by the coming of war.

Yet as the English coast receded, Marlborough's thoughts dwelt not on the awesome responsibilities ahead of him, but on Sarah:

It is impossible to express with what a heavy heart I parted from you when I was by the water's side. I could have given my life to come back . . . I did for a great while, with a perspective glass [telescope], look upon the cliffs, in hopes I might have had one sight of you. We are now out of sight of Margate, and I have neither soul nor spirits, but I do at this time suffer so much that nothing but being with you can recompense it. I pray to God to make you and yours happy; and if I could contribute anything to it with the utmost hazard of my life, I should be glad to do it.

Sarah Churchill; oil sketch c. 1690-95 by Sir Godfrey Kneller

In The Hague Marlborough took up the burden of duty he was to carry for nine years. On him rested the task of leading a coalition of second-rank powers against France, the super-power of the age. And France's strategy was directed by one man, Louis XIV. Marlborough on the other hand had all the problems of getting allies to agree. He was to carry far more daunting responsibilities than Wellington did, for whereas Wellington for most of the time was to conduct a single campaign in a subsidiary theatre – Spain – Marlborough had to run the entire war. He was a kind of combined Winston Churchill and Dwight Eisenhower, except that he was never to enjoy their authority. For the Dutch flatly refused to make him allied generalissimo with full powers. Instead he had

Queen Anne, attributed to Kneller

to command by persuasion – by sheer force of personality. And what this was going to cost him in mental wear and tear he discovered as soon as he joined the allied Army at Nijmegen on the Meuse to begin his first campaign.

It was an eighteenth-century Nato – English, Dutch, Germans, Danes. The Dutch leaders, remembering past French invasions of their homeland, could think of nothing but standing passively on the defensive against the French army on the Meuse under Marshal Boufflers. Marlborough himself wanted to launch a bold southward stroke against Boufflers' communications, so forcing the French commander to retreat. Best of all, he wanted to defeat Boufflers in a great battle, which would transform the war at a stroke. Marlborough found himself engaged in endless brain-heating argument with his Dutch colleagues before his every move, for, cautious and mistrusting, they feared to take risks. On three separate occasions in that first campaign he succeeded in man-oeuvring the French into his hands – and each time the Dutch leaders either forbade him to attack or delayed a decision until it was too late. Outwardly Marlborough maintained a superhuman patience and cour-tesy; inwardly he seethed with frustration. After one such lost victory he wrote to his friend Lord Godolphin, the Lord Treasurer and head of the government at home: 'I am in so ill-humour that I dare not trust myself to write more, but believe this truth, that I honour and love you, my lady Marl, and my children and I would die for the Queen.'

Nevertheless by sheer patient tenacity, by force of personality and will, he dragged the Dutch up the Meuse, taking fortress after fortress. When the campaign ended in the autumn Marlborough had captured more territory than William of Orange ever had in any single year.

But it almost proved to be his last campaign. On his way back to The Hague by boat, he was ambushed on the Meuse by a French raiding party. Luckily a servant happened to have a French passport made out to his brother General Charles Churchill according to the civilised custom of the time. In the dim lantern light Marlborough was able to pass himself off as his brother.

Queen Anne herself was delighted with Marlborough's achievements. She welcomed him home with a dukedom. It was, however, typical of John's and Sarah's shrewdness that they were reluctant to accept the title until an income was granted to support it in proper style.

They had reached the top at last; taken their place among the great nobility of England. Their daughters were all to make splendid mar-riages. But their hopes for carrying on their new title lay in their only son Jack, now Lord Churchill, aged sixteen, an undergraduate at King's College, Cambridge.

In February 1703 Jack went down with smallpox, the most dreaded disease of the period. 'I am so troubled at the sad condition this poor child seems to be in,' wrote the Duke to Sarah in his anguish, 'that I know not what to do. I pray God to give you some comfort in this great affliction . . . ' On 20 February Jack died. John and Sarah had not only lost a dearly loved son, but also the keystone of their patient ambition. All through the 1703 campaign Marlborough carried a double burden of private grief and the cares of command. How deep that grief was we know from a letter he wrote after seeing a Corpus Christi Day procession in Cologne: 'The thought how pleased Lord Churchill would have been with such a sight has added much to my uneasiness. Since it has pleased God to take him, I do wish from my soul I could think less of him.'

He was also profoundly worried about Sarah's health. She had thought that she was pregnant again, but in fact both her mental and physical balance had been affected by her grief. From his camps on the march Marlborough poured out his anxiety to her by letter:

I shall have no rest till I hear again from you, for your health is much dearer to me than my own . . . For God's sake let me know exactly how you are; and if you think my being with you can do you any good, you shall quickly see you are much dearer to me than fame.

It was another campaign of appalling frustration at the hands of the Dutch. He sought to break through the lines of the Brabant, the French field fortifications protecting the Spanish Netherlands (modern Belgium), by a feint attack near Namur, followed by an offensive near Antwerp. The Dutch commanders bungled that offensive, and thereafter simply obstructed every plan he put forward. With a savagely sardonic humour the Duke wrote to Godolphin in August that 'I shall not be very fond of staying with an army that is to do nothing but eat forage.' For all his self-control he finally reached a state of utter desperation, as is revealed by a private letter to the head of the Dutch government, Antonie Heinsius: 'If I might have millions given me to serve another year and be obliged to do nothing but by the unanimous consent of the generals, I would much sooner die . . . '

By the end of the 1703 campaign Marlborough had come to a momentous decision – next year he would campaign in south Germany. In the first place, this would free him from the shackles of the Dutch. But, more important, it was the only way of saving his other major ally, the Habsburg Empire. All through 1703 French armies had been pushing the Habsburg forces back. Bavaria had now joined the war on the French side. It seemed all too probable that the French and the Bavarians might be able to advance along the Danube in 1704 to Vienna, the capital of the Habsburg

Empire, and there dictate peace. This would spell the finish of the alliance.

The Duke's new strategy was grand but simple. Hitherto the allies had fought in two main theatres far apart – the English and Dutch in the Low Countries, and the Habsburg Empire and Baden in southern Germany. Now he meant to unite the bulk of the allied forces in one theatre only – on the Danube. In the Low Countries he would merely stand on the defensive. The real test, however, lay in the carrying-out. And this demanded the whole range of Marlborough's talents; that range which makes him pre-eminent among British commanders.

First during the winter of 1703-4 he played the politician and diplomat. He persuaded his government colleagues in London to back his strategy. He made secret arrangements with the Habsburg ambassador, whom he promised to march his army half across Europe to the Habsburg Empire's rescue, providing the Habsburg forces which linked up with him were commanded by the Habsburgs' best soldier, Prince Eugène. He persuaded Queen Anne to give him *carte blanche* to act in her name as he saw fit.

In April 1704 he sailed from England to undertake his boldest and riskiest campaign. He therefore needed Sarah's love and support more than ever in his life. Instead she had accused him of being unfaithful. There was no truth in the accusation; it was the sad fantasy of an emotionally disturbed middle-aged woman. A tragic letter from the Duke to Sarah survives from his last weeks in England:

If the thought of the children we have had, or aught else that has ever been dear between us, can oblige you to be so good-natured as not to leave bed for the remaining time, I shall take it kindly to my dying day, and do most faithfully promise you that I will take the first occasion of leaving England, and assure you that you may rest quiet from that time you shall never more be troubled with my hated sight.

It was only after Marlborough had returned to his official residence in The Hague, the Mauritshuis, that a repentant letter from Sarah at last eased his mind. 'You have by your kindness,' he replied to her, 'preserved my quiet and I believe my life. For till I received this letter I have been very indifferent of what should become of myself.'

In The Hague the Duke bluntly told the Dutch leaders that he had the Queen's authority to march to 'the Moselle'; with typical cunning he made no mention of his true objective, the much further off Danube. The Dutch could only cave in and agree to cooperate. Marlborough the statesman had done his work; now it was all up to Marlborough the soldier. As he wrote to Godolphin, 'I am very aware that I take a great deal upon me.' In fact he was taking on nothing less than the fate of Europe.

On 20 May the army struck camp at Bedburg, north-west of Cologne, and set off on the long march to the Danube – sixty battalions of infantry, forty-six squadrons of cavalry, carts, guns, wagons. Other contingents were to join later along the route.

The march was a tremendous test of Marlborough's skill as an organiser. For some 250 miles over bad roads, through mountains and across rivers lacking permanent bridges he had to move and feed the equivalent of the combined populations of the then two largest cities in England after London. On equivalent marches a hundred years later Napoleon's troops went starving and barefoot. Marlborough on the other hand had everything prepared in advance to the last detail. Ad Captain Parker of Hamilton's Regiment records in his memoirs:

As we marched through the countries of our allies, commissaries were appointed to furnish us with all manner of necessaries for man and horse; these were brought to the [camping] ground before we arrived, and the soldiers had nothing to do but pitch their tents, boil their kettles, and lie down to rest. Surely never was such a march carried on with more order and regularity, and less fatigue both to man and horse.

Soon the Duke learned that one large French army was following him from the Low Countries; others lay somewhere ahead of him; and still some 200 miles to go. The risks were immense – a lost battle against overwhelming numbers before he could join his allies; the defeat of the Habsburg Empire; the exposure of the Netherlands to invasion.

On 25 May he reached Coblenz, where the Rhine is joined by the Moselle. The French now expected him to turn up the Moselle in order to invade France via Lorraine. Instead he crossed over the Moselle, marched through Coblenz itself and arrived again on the bank of the Rhine. Here his troops found a bridge of boats – as pre-arranged by the Duke back in the winter. The army crossed the Rhine to the east bank and marched on to the south.

On 27 May, at Braubach, he turned away from the Rhine into the Taunus Mountains. The hitherto fine weather broke. Mud brought him new problems, as he reported to the Dutch government: 'There has been so great rains that the artillery and bread wagons were two whole days getting up the mountain this side of Coblenz.' The French, however, had bigger problems. For Marlborough's skill as a strategist had left them bereft of the initiative; haplessly groping in the dark. He had tricked them into thinking he was going up the Moselle. Now he tricked them again into believing he meant to march on southwards and invade France via Alsace. They gathered their armies to block this move. But the Duke had sold them another dummy, leaving them all in the wrong places. On 6 June, at Wiesloch, he swung east, towards the Danube.

Prince Eugène of Savoy

On 10 June in the little village of Mundelsheim amid terraced vine-yards, the Duke first met Prince Eugène, the Habsburg commander, who rode over to confer. That evening the Duke entertained Eugène to a grand banquet splendidly graced by the Marlborough campaign silver. It was the beginning of one of the most remarkable comradeships in war; Marlborough older but less experienced, Eugène a veteran at forty-one.

On 27 June Marlborough completed his long march at Giengen, north-east of Ulm on the Danube, linking up with the Margrave of Baden's army and other contingents. The allied commanders were amazed to see Marlborough's soldiers and horses in such superb con-dition after so long a march.

The Duke had now concentrated in the Danube theatre the largest army so far seen in the war. He and his colleagues decided that their first task must be to invade Bavaria and compel its Elector to desert the French and make peace. On 2 July Donauworth, a key fortress commanding the Danube crossing, fell after Marlborough had taken the Schellenberg, a fortified hill overlooking the town, in savage and costly fighting. But there followed a month of disappointment and setback. The Habsburg Emperor defaulted on his promise of heavy guns – and without heavy guns Marlborough could not besiege Bavarian cities. Instead he was forced to resort to a campaign of terror against the population in order to persuade the Elector to peace – the burning of farms and villages. 'This is so contrary to my nature,' the Duke wrote to Sarah, 'that nothing but absolute necessity could have obliged me to consent to it.'

It proved all in vain. After a month of complicated manoeuvring, two French armies, under Marshals Tallard and Marsin, and the Bavarian army succeeded in uniting south of the Danube. They decided to advance northward across the Danube, attack the outnumbered Eugène and then cut Marlborough's communications. They failed to realise how closely Eugène and Marlborough were in touch. On 10 August Marlborough ordered his army to march to join Eugène. On the morning of the 12th Eugène and the Duke climbed the tower of Tapfheim church to look for the enemy over to the westward. Through their telescopes they could see the French and Bavarians swarming over the distant plain, obviously about to make camp, 'whereupon,' in the Duke's words, 'we resolved to attack them'.

That night after tap-to Marlborough fell on his knees in his tent and prayed. He knew all too well how much hung on this battle – for England, for Europe, for himself personally.

Early in the morning of 13 August 1704 the Duke and Eugène rode forward with the advanced guard to reconnoitre. At first it was misty, but as the sun grew hotter the mist quickly cleared. It was going to be a blazing hot day. From high ground to the east of the French camp the allied commanders could see its tents stretching across a level plain ahead of them. The French position was immensely strong. One flank rested on the village of Blenheim and on the Danube just beyond it. A stream, the Nebel, protected the French line where it stretched across the plain. Though today no more than a narrow dyke, the Nebel was then about twelve feet wide and very boggy: a major obstacle to the clumsy parade-ground formations of the period. The French centre was protected by another village, Oberglau, which the French hastily barricaded as they had Blenheim. Their left flank, which Prince Eugène was going to attack, stretched away to the village of Lutzingen, also protected by the stream and by rough, scrubby ground. Wooded hills beyond Lutzingen made it impossible to outflank the enemy on that side either. One of the Duke's generals said that if he had been in command, he would not have dared to attack.

This was the very first time that Marlborough had commanded an army in a great battle – and opposite him lay the most renowned army in Europe, with a record of forty years of victory. Yet Marlborough had won the first trick, taking the French commander, Tallard, by surprise. Tallard had been certain that the allies were about to retreat, not attack. His deployment took place in a frantic scramble.

The allied commanders had some 56,000 men to get into position along nearly five miles of battle-line – British, Dutch, Danes and Germans. Of the total the British themselves numbered only 9000. Standard drill had yet to be evolved, so that the armies of the period were cumbersome instruments. Deployment was more like an exercise in crowd control than the precise movements of the modern Guards on parade. It was well into mid-morning before Marlborough had completed his deployment along the eastern side of the Nebel. Since Prince Eugène had much further to go, it was not until past midday that he was ready to attack. In the meantime the Duke and his soldiers had to endure the French cannonfire sweeping across the open ground. There was a drumhead service to fortify the soul, followed by martial music to rouse the fighting spirit. The Duke's chaplain, Dr Hare, who was present, records:

His Grace now rode along the lines to observe the posture and countenance of his men, and found both them and all officers of the allied army very cheerful and impatient of coming to a closer engagement with the enemy. As he was passing in front of the first line a large cannon ball grazed upon a ploughed land, close by his horse's side, and almost covered him with dust. He never halted his pace for this, but moved on.

At about 12.30 a messenger came from Prince Eugène to say that he was ready. Marlborough swung himself into the saddle and rode off to direct the attack on Blenheim village in person.

The attack went in across the Nebel, past water-mills set alight by the French and over swampy ground towards Blenheim's church-spire; infantry, guns and cavalry working together. The outskirts of Blenheim billowed French powder smoke; there was charge and counter-charge. But Marlborough, on the spot, exploited each passing opportunity, personally ordering his units forward into action. Steadily the English forced the enemy garrison back. In desperation the French kept feeding in reinforcements, until finally most of Tallard's infantry became locked up inside Blenheim, so weakening the rest of his front – as the Duke intended.

But Blenheim itself constituted only one sector in a nearly five-mile-long battle-line. Neither commander could see the whole battlefield from one point because of folds in the ground and the reeking fog from the black gunpowder. And these armies of around 60,000 men could only be directed by means of bugle or trumpet calls, or aides-de-camp galloping about with orders trying to find the units the orders were meant for. Control of an early eighteenth-century battle offered a supreme test of leadership, willpower and sheer tactical instinct.

Tallard, the French commander, lost grip very early on. His units fought where they stood in a struggle without a theme. But Marlborough was always managing to turn up at exactly the point where he was most needed, either to plug a gap or organise a swift counter-attack. In this way he kept a personal grasp on the entire floundering scene of violence. Amid the racket and turmoil he remained cool-nerved and cool-headed. Once he came upon an officer falling back with his men, and told him with an ironic politeness that was typical of him: 'You are under a mistake, the enemy lies that way; you have nothing to do but face him and the day is your own.'

All through the hot afternoon the Duke was gradually moulding victory out of the chaos of battle. His attacks on Blenheim and then on Oberlau bottled up their garrisons and induced Tallard to thin out his centre. And it was here that he meant eventually to break through. A powerful force of his cavalry and infantry made their way across the marshy Nebel stream over causeways of brushwood laid by the engineers, and formed up in a sweep of open stubble-field.

Tallard has thus allowed the Duke to establish overwhelming strength on the French side of the stream. For while this advance was in progress, the French cavalry simply watched from the crestline of the slope beyond; a fatal error. Too late Tallard launched his squadrons in a grand attack aimed at driving Marlborough back into the Nebel. But Marlborough ordered his own cavalry to retire behind his infantry. The French horsemen were brought to a halt by rolling musket volleys and cannon firing case-shot (metal canisters filled with scrap-iron).

Now Marlborough rode along his line. He saw that the enemy were wavering, and he ordered his own cavalry to charge. The French fired one wavering volley from their carbines and fled – even the crack household troops, the *Maison du Roi*. Such was the confusion that, in their panic flight many French troopers rode over the bank of the Danube and drowned themselves. Tallard was taken prisoner in the press of fugitives. Meanwhile Eugène by valiantly attacking throughout the day had

The taking of Marshall Tallard at the Battle of Blenheim; tapestry from Blenheim Palace

John Churchill by John Riley (1646-1691)

prevented the superior numbers in front of him going to Tallard's aid.

When the surrounded garrison of Blenheim surrendered that evening the Duke's triumph was complete. But he himself was now utterly spent after seventeen hours in the saddle; seventeen hours at full stretch both mentally and physically, rather like an athlete and a chess grand-master combined, but with the added strain of danger and leadership.

Nevertheless, he managed to scribble a note to Sarah on the back of a tavern reckoning, the first piece of paper to come to hand: 'I have not time to say more but to beg you will give my humble duty to the Queen and let her know her army has had a glorious victory. Monsieur Tallard and two other generals are in my coach and I am following the rest.'

Tallard's army had been utterly destroyed. Yet – a sign of the bloodiness of the close-quarters fighting of the time – the allied losses in that single day equalled the Eighth Army's losses in the eleven days of the Second Battle of Alamein in October 1942.

If the battle probed Marlborough's qualities as a fighting commander, the aftermath revealed him as a man. He paid a personal visit to Tallard, who had lost a son on the field, and, as his chaplain narrates, 'His grace desired to know how far it was in his power to make him easy under his misfortune, offering at the same time the convenience of his quarters and to take him thither in his coach.' In the days that followed, Marlborough suffered a spiritual hangover after the violence, carnage and strain. As he wrote to Lord Godolphin, the Lord Treasurer: 'Ever since the battle I have been so employed about our own wounded men and the prisoners that I have not had one hour's quiet, which has so disordered me that were I in London I should be in bed with a high fever.'

In Paris Louis XIV and his court had just been celebrating the birth of a grandson. Gradually news of the catastrophe to French arms trickled through. At first there was disbelief that a French army could suffer so great a defeat; then, dismay. It was like the impact of Vietnam on America, but all at once. After forty years of conquest Louis XIV had been robbed of the initiative. The legend of his invincibility lay smashed. The whole climate of the war had been changed, for it was now France, not the Habsburg Empire, which lay under threat.

In England the people celebrated Blenheim with church-bells and beer, rejoicing in England's first great victory on land since Agincourt. And when the Duke returned home that autumn at the end of the campaign, the grateful Queen crowned his triumph by giving him the royal manor of Woodstock, near Oxford, there to build at royal expense a great mansion.

How did so much fame, such tremendous success, affect Marlborough? John Evelyn, the diarist and an old acquaintance of his, who met him by chance at this time, recorded that he 'took me by the hand with extraordinary familiarity and civility, as formerly he used to do, without any alteration of his good nature. I had not seen him for some years and believed he might have forgotten me.'

Marlborough hoped that 1705 might bring final victory. He planned to invade France down the Moselle valley, via Lorraine. But instead he experienced bitter frustration and disappointment. His allies failed to keep their promises to join him in the field by the agreed time, and Louis XIV, who knew none of the anxieties and problems of an allied generalis-simo, was able to block Marlborough's intended advance while at the same time threatening the Netherlands. The Duke was forced to march his army back to the Low Countries – a major strategic setback. The night the army set off he gave vent to his inner anguish to Sarah in a letter: 'My dearest soul, pity me and love me.'

Now he found himself back amid the scenes of all his frustrations of 1702-3, the Belgian Plain; back under the constraints of obstructive Dutch generals still suspicious of his leadership and fearful of risk. His one success of the campaign was to break through the French Lines of Brabant by a complex but highly Marlburian double deception – of his own allies as well as the French. He put in the real attack where earlier he had put in an obviously feint attack; the apparently 'real' attack, allotted to the Dutch, being in fact the true feint.

Yet such indecisive and disappointing campaigns tell much about Marlborough the man. Though outwardly always so calm, courteous and patient, he was inwardly tortured by the curbing of his dynamism by his colleagues; maddened with frustration when his schemes were blocked by the cautious and unimaginative. A man of sensitive feelings and often depressed, he poured it all out in his letters to Sarah. In one letter during the 1705 campaign he told her: 'But really my spirit is so broke that whenever I can get from this employment I must live quietly or die. It is most certain that on many occasions I have the spleen and am weary of my life.'

The strain of controlling his feelings in public under all the pro-vocations led to splitting headaches and eyestrain – very likely psy-chological, as he himself told Sarah: 'I own you my sickness comes from fretting.' His correspondence with Sarah far off in England constituted his mental refuge; sitting in camp writing by candlelight, he reached out for her. 'I am very uneasy,' he once wrote, 'when your letters do not come regularly, for without flattery my greatest support are these thoughts I have of your kindness.'

The beginning of the 1706 campaign found Marlborough still sunk in despondency. 'God knows,' he wrote, 'I go with a heavy heart, for I have no hope of doing anything considerable unless the French do what I am confident they will not . . . ' For once again his allies had defaulted on their promises, their troops arriving too late for the Duke to carry out the most ambitious strategic plan of his whole career – nothing less than marching his army all the way from the Netherlands to Northern Italy, there to join Prince Eugène and invade France via Savoy. Instead, he had to abandon the project, and reconcile himself to another year in the Low Countries trying to bring the evasive French to battle and arguing endlessly with the Dutch.

But on 18 May 1706 news came that the French army under the Marshal de Villeroi was advancing – in fact, under orders from Louis XIV to fight a battle. Marlborough's mood swung from gloom to elation. He wrote to his friend Lord Godolphin, 'They pretend to be stronger both in horse and foot; but, with the blessing of God, I hope for success, being resolved to venture . . . '

The armies met at Ramillies, south-east of Brussels, on 23 May. In many ways the battle was a re-play of Blenheim; the battlefields themselves astonishingly alike. Once again the Duke seized the initiative at the very outset by attacking, so imposing his will on the enemy commander. He launched his redcoats across a stream against the French left flank. Villeroi thinned his centre in order to send reinforcements to repel this attack – just as Marlborough intended. The Duke then withdrew his forces across the stream, but left a part of them visible on the slope opposite the French position as a constant threat. The remainder he switched to his centre under cover of the sloping ground – and it was in the centre that he meant to break through, just as at Blenheim.

But the French fought stoutly, bringing the first allied charge to a halt and successfully counter-charging. There was a ferocious mêlée – rather like a modern street riot, but fought with deadly weapons. The Duke himself, in the thick of the struggle as always, was nearly ridden down by the French cavalry when his horse stumbled at a ditch and threw him. He was rescued by two battalions of Swiss mercenaries. Gradually the sheer superiority of numbers Marlborough had created in the centre proved decisive. At about 4 pm he launched his final charge, and the French centre and right gave way altogether. The entire plain was covered with fugitives as Villeroi's army broke up in rout.

On 28 May 1706 the Duke rode as a conqueror into the Grand' Place at Brussels, then the capital of the Spanish Netherlands. In the fourteenth-century Hotel de Ville, the city fathers acknowledged the allied candidate for the Spanish throne, Charles III, as their king. There were honours and feasting. But Marlborough confessed to Sarah that he could not yet take pleasure in his victory – and for a familiar enough reason: 'I have been in so continual a hurry since the battle of Ramillies, by which my blood is so heated that when I go to bed I sleep so unquietly that I cannot get rid of my headache.'

The complete structure of French power in the Spanish Netherlands now collapsed. As Marlborough wrote, 'We are now masters of Ghent and tomorrow I shall send some troops to Bruges. So many towns have submitted since the battle that it really looks more like a dream than truth.' Queen Anne breathlessly wrote to her Captain-General, 'Mr Freeman': 'It is impossible for me ever to say so much as I ought in return of your great and faithful services to me but I will endeavour by all the actions of my life to show how truly sensible [aware] I am of them.'

By the end of the campaign Marlborough had conquered almost the whole of the Spanish Netherlands. Now Louis XIV's own dominions lay before him. When he returned to England that December to be cheered and fêted, he stood on the summit of his success, the greatest living soldier.

Although his hair under the great wig had for the most part turned grey, his face remained surprisingly youthful for a man of fifty-six. Even the pompous portraits of the time reveal more than hint of leashed dynamism of his nature; strength blended with sensuality in the lines of the mouth. A Dutch colleague, Sicco van Goslinga, who was at the Duke's side throughout the Ramillies campaign, has left this pen picture of him:

He is above average height and with as fine a figure as you could see; he has a flawlessly handsome face; fine, flashing eyes, with a clear red and white complexion which could put the fair sex to shame; good teeth . . . He has plenty of good sense and sensibility, shrewd and sound judgement, keen and deep understanding, is a good judge of men . . . He has a very gracious manner, and if his handsome and prepossessing countenance disposes everyone in his favour, his manners and gentleness captivate all who are biased against him or displeased with him.

These were the personal qualities that enabled him to keep the various members of the ramshackle alliance together year after year; that won him the trust and loyalty of the officers and soldiers of his international army; and to which only some jealous and suspicious Dutch leaders seemed immune. Yet his natural charm shaded into something else – a means of hiding his purposes, a tool for manipulating others. As van Goslinga wrote, 'He is a man of deep dissimulation, all the more dangerous because he disguises it in a manner and style of expression which appears to convey nothing but candour itself.'

The Duke now kept up immense personal state, causing some to accuse him of vanity. But this was an age of ceremony, so that the maintenance of a proper dignity was a personal and political necessity. After all, he, the son of an obscure squire, had to lead kings, princes and dukes. He himself was now a Prince of the Holy Roman Empire, so honoured as a reward after Blenheim by the Holy Roman Emperor. Nevertheless he lived simply enough in the field, often preferring to eat at the tables of his subordinates – one way of keeping his finger on the army's pulse.

His critics however alleged colossal meanness as well as avarice. There is no doubt that both as a private individual and head of the army he counted pennies and hated waste – the deeply-branded lesson of poverty in early life and the example of his spendthrift father. According to one story, when his linen gaiters got soaked by rain one day and could not be removed without tearing, he told his servants to take care to rip them down the seams, so that they could be sewn up again.

As a father he was fond and indulgent, caught like many another in the cross-fire between his daughters and a wife indignant about their rudeness to her. Once in the middle of a campaign he replied to Sarah's complaints about them: 'Hitherto I really have not had time to write to my children, but when I do, be assured that I shall let them know my heart as to their living dutifully and kindly with you, and let me beg for my sake of my dear soul [as he called Sarah] that she will pass by little faults and consider that they are but very young.'

The building of Blenheim Palace gave him a fresh mental escape. Designed by Sir John Vanbrugh, it is one of the few baroque masterpieces in England. Sarah herself would have rather had a more domestic, comfortable house in the style of Sir Christopher Wren – but then she missed the whole point of Vanbrugh's conception. For Vanbrugh was not seeking to design a homely country-house of the kind that English people like best even today, but to proclaim Marlborough's triumph in stone.

At the Duke's request Parliament passed an Act so that his title could descend through the female line, and Blenheim Palace and its estate were made inseparable from the title. So at last John and Sarah had accomplished their ambition: they had founded a great landed family that would carry their name down the centuries. All the prizes he had striven for now seemed to be his. But in fact the foundations of his career were already slipping, and slipping where they had originally been laid, at Court.

The cause lay in an intricate pavane of political and personal intrigue with the Queen at its centre. For the Queen was no longer the Marlboroughs' loving friend, but cold and distant. Lord Godolphin, the Lord Treasurer and head of the government at home, and the Marlboroughs kept urging Queen Anne to appoint Whig ministers to high office because her government needed Whig votes in Parliament. And Sarah's urging took the form of endless shrill, bullying argument. She was a female politician before her time. But the Queen hated the Whigs and was afraid of falling under party domination. The more Godolphin and the Marlboroughs pressed her to appoint Whigs, the more they alienated her.

Instead she turned to new friends within her household, Abigail Hill, later Mrs Masham, a Lady of the Bedchamber – soft, gentle, sly. The last of the dancers in this pavane of intrigue was Robert Harley, the Tory Secretary of State and a close colleague of Godolphin and Marlborough. Apart from genuine differences over policy with his colleagues, Harley wanted Godolphin's job. He was even slier than Abigail – who was his distant cousin, his close confidante and his private link to the Queen.

The pavane danced on until Marlborough came home at the end of the 1707 campaign, when he and Godolphin decided on a show-down. Either Harley went or they did. The Duke wrote to the Queen, once so close a friend:

I find myself obliged to have so much regard to my own honour and reputation as not to be every day made a sacrifice to falsehood and treachery but most humbly to acquaint your majesty that no consideration can make me serve any longer with that man. And I beseech your majesty to look upon me from this moment as forced out of service as long as you think fit to continue him in it.

On 19 February 1708 the customary Sunday morning meeting of the Cabinet Council took place in St James's Palace. The Queen was at the head of the table; Harley by her side. But Marlborough and Godolphin were not present. The other Council members refused to go on with the meeting without them. Anne, furious and humiliated, left the room. Next day she admitted defeat and dismissed Harley.

But she never forgave or forgot. The old intimacy with the Marlboroughs had been destroyed, even though a façade of friendship was still preserved. And Harley still retained his influence – via the backstairs and Abigail, plumping the royal pillows. Harley, like Anne herself, was bent on ultimate revenge.

Deprived of the Queen's loyal support, Marlborough was to find his own position grow more and more shaky, for it now rested on his own prestige alone. And 1707 had proved another disappointing year in the field, just like 1705, the campaign that followed his first great victory at Blenheim. An attempt by Prince Eugène to invade France along the Riviera coast ended in failure, while in Spain the allies had been crushingly defeated at Almanza. Marlborough's own efforts to cap Ramillies with another battle in the Low Countries had been frustrated by the new French commander Vendôme, who sheltered among the French frontier fortresses and evaded action. Peace still seemed far off, and the grand alliance began to show signs of disintegration. In 1708 the Duke therefore sought an answer to all his problems in a fresh victory in the field.

However, Prince Eugène was late in joining him in the Low Countries as arranged, and the French were able to strike first, pouncing on the fortresses of Bruges and Ghent, where traitors opened the gates to them. It was the only occasion in the war when the French caught Marlborough with his breeches down. The shock hit him the harder because he happened to be suffering from a fever at the time, and for once he lost his famous calm; indeed, he suffered a kind of temporary moral collapse. A Prussian officer on his staff recorded that the Duke 'felt his misfortune so keenly that I believed he would succumb to his grief as he was so seized by it that he was afraid of being suffocated'.

Nevertheless Marlborough swiftly recovered. As often with him a bout of depression served as a prelude to dynamic action and brilliant feats of generalship. He learned that the French were marching on Lessines, and rightly guessed that the fortress of Oudenarde would be next. He therefore raced the French for Lessines, forcing them to turn away to the north-west; then raced them for Oudenarde itself. For he knew that if Oudenarde fell, he would be virtually cut off from the North Sea coast. At daybreak on 11 July 1708 the Duke despatched General Cadogan to Oudenarde with an advanced guard with orders to seize the high ground beyond the River Scheldt and intercept the French march. By about 10.30 am Cadogan was over the Scheldt near Oudernarde by pontoon-bridge. The Duke himself ordered the main body to 'step out' so as to reach Cadogan before he could be overwhelmed by French numbers. The troops 'stepped out'. 'It was not a march,' wrote Goslinga, 'it was a race.'

When Marlborough reached high ground just east of Oudenarde, he saw the dust-cloud kicked up by the advancing French over to the north, beyond the Scheldt. He rode forward to take personal command of operations. The French army under Marshal Vendôme and the royal Duke of Burgundy deployed facing south along a wooded crestline buttressed with villages. The Duke judged it 'as strong a post as is possible to be found'. Yet he decided to attack, even though the allied army was only arriving piecemeal – probably the boldest decision of his career. In his own words later, 'I was positively resolved to endeavour by all means a battle, thinking that nothing else would make the Queen's business go well . . . this reason only made me venture this battle, otherwise I did give the enemy too much advantage.'

In close, rather English-looking countryside of woods and fields, a fierce encounter battle developed, swaying this way and that as each side fed in fresh troops as they came up. It displayed the Duke at his best as a fighting commander – cool-headed, quick-thinking; with an instinctive sense for the run of the struggle. Finally he ordered a large force of allied cavalry to sweep round to the west of the fighting line and take the French in the rear. The stroke was completely successful. Only a portion of the French army which had not advanced against the allies succeeded in escaping the ring of fire drawn by the Duke.

Next morning the Duke and Prince Eugène rode into the Market Square of Oudenarde to view the throng of French prisoners. Enemy losses amounted to 20,000 men; the surviving French forces were utterly demoralised.

Oudenarde constituted Marlborough's most original victory – an interception off the march and an encounter battle, instead of the parade-ground line-up usual at the period.

However, this time the Thanksgiving Service at St Paul's was the occasion of a blazing row between the Queen and Sarah. It began on the way in the coach, when Sarah accused the Queen of not wearing the jewels which she, Sarah, as Mistress of the Robes, had laid out for her. It was, cried Sarah, deliberately done as an affront on her husband's great day; more, done at Abigail's instigation. The climax of the quarrel took place in public on the steps of the cathedral, when Sarah actually told her sovereign to 'be quiet!' It marked the finish of 'Mrs Morley' and 'Mrs Freeman'. In future the two women met only on official business. To the Duke – 'Mr Freeman' – this was a fateful development because it meant that his power-base at home was crumbling away just at the time when in the field he seemed at last in sight of final victory. For after Oudenarde France now lay open to invasion.

Marlborough now conceived a strategy incredibly daring for that age of warfare – to bypass the French frontier fortresses and, in conjunction with a seaborne combined operation to seize a base on the Channel coast, march straight on Paris. Prince Eugène and other allied commanders believed the scheme to be too risky, and they may well have been right. The allies could have found themselves entangled in a delaying war deep in the heart of France – just as was soon to happen to Charles XII of Sweden when he invaded Russia.

Instead the allies decided on a step-by-step invasion, clearing a secure path through the zone of fortresses that lay along France's northern frontier. They began in August 1708 with Lille, the most powerful of them all, the great military engineer Vauban's masterpiece; layer upon layer of massive ramparts and moats. While Marlborough fended off a relieving French army, Eugène conducted the siege itself, pounding away with immense quantities of powder and shot to bring down Vauban's masonry. The siege dragged on and on; when Eugène was wounded leading an assault the Duke had to take charge of the siege in person, only

The Siege of Lille, 1708; engraving of 1736

to find that there remained only four days' supply of ammunition. He reported home: 'I cannot prove what I am going to say; I really believe we have been from the very beginning of the siege betrayed; for a great part of our stores have been embezzled.' Now he had the entire anxiety of the operations at Lille on his mind as well as the flow of bad news from home.

Only a special convoy of ammunition wagons from Ostend, which fought its way through a French ambush, saved the siege. Gradually the allies pounded their way in, forcing the French fortress commander, Marshal Boufflers, to retire into the Citadel, the most formidable obstacle of all. At last, on 9 December, Boufflers surrendered, marching out of a gateway bearing Louis XIV's coat of arms with the full honours of war;

another shattering setback for his royal master at Marlborough's hands.

But as 1708 turned to 1709 an even worse calamity than the Duke's hammer-blows befell France – the most dreadful winter in European memory. Sentinels froze to death at their posts. There was an ice fair on the Thames; ice-floes in the Channel. To the French people, already impoverished by war, the cold brought famine. Louis XIV recognised that France must have peace. In the spring, while snow gave way to appallingly wet weather that drowned the young crops, peace talks opened in the Netherlands.

By May peace seemed a certainty, for the French had agreed to almost all the allied terms. But Louis refused to accept two particular conditions that amounted to his complete humiliation, indeed virtual surrender. The allies therefore had now to make a choice whether to accept a compromise or fight on for their complete war aims. The Dutch and the Habsburg Emperor wanted a compromise. But the British Government (England and Scotland had become the United Kingdom of Great Britain in 1707) was now dominated by the Whig ministers Queen Anne had been forced to accept. And the Whigs were the 'hawks' of the period, determined to inflict a humiliating surrender on Louis XIV.

Marlborough's personal role in the peace negotiations was crucial, because although he was no longer as powerful a man as he had once been, he still enjoyed immense prestige. He himself favoured a compromise peace. If he had taken a public stand on the issue, it might therefore have proved decisive. Instead he funked – it is not too strong a word – such a role, and limited himself to hints and advice behind the scenes, acting as if he were no more than a mere instrument of the Whig ministers in London. But why? The answer seems to be that he simply did not like expressing a minority point of view. As he confided to his friend Godolphin, 'I do not love to be singular, especially when it was doing what France seemed to desire.' Back in 1685, during the Sedgemoor campaign, he had taken a similar attitude, writing to a minister: 'I am afraid of giving my opinion freely for fear that it should not agree with what is the king's intentions, and so only expose myself.' Here is another facet of a complex character – an appeasing streak oddly out of keeping with his strength and resolution in the field.

In the face of Whig demands for nothing less than all the allied conditions, the peace talks broke down. The war dragged on, a matter now of sieges aimed at forcing Louis into fresh negotiations. And while the Duke campaigned, letters kept arriving from Sarah indignantly complaining about the Queen's treatment of her and nagging at him to write to the Queen on her behalf. In fact the bitterness that now lay between the two women was largely Sarah's own fault, for in middle age she had turned into a shrill, bullying virago who had quarrelled with everybody, including her own daughters, including the architect of Blenheim Palace. Queen Anne herself, no longer the shy, unsure child Sarah had first known, was, though Sarah seemed to find it hard to remember, Queen of England and a woman of immense strength of character. Anne did not therefore take kindly to Sarah's nagging reproaches. When the Duke at last dutifully wrote to her on Sarah's behalf, the Queen replied:

You seem dissatisfied with my behaviour to the Duchess of Marlborough. I do not love complaining, but it is impossible to help saying on this occasion I believe nobody was ever so used by a friend as I have been ever since my coming to the crown. I desire nothing but that she would leave off teasing me and tormenting me, and behave herself with the decency she ought both to her friend and Queen, and this I hope you will do.

For Marlborough personally it was an added strain to suffer a conflict of loyalties between the two women round whom his whole career had revolved. In September 1709 he was actually in the middle of writing a soothing reply to Sarah's most recent diatribe when news came that the French were on the march, apparently seeking battle.

The French army, under the command of its two best soldiers Boufflers and Villars, advanced as far as Malplaquet, a few miles south-west of Mons, a fortress Marlborough and Eugène had just besieged. Just beyond the village of Malplaquet the enemy dug themselves in for battle, their flanks resting in thick woods, their centre in the open ground between, protected by ramparts of hewn logs chained together. The French army and nation had been rendered desperate but resolute by the humiliating allied peace terms. Marlborough himself was now weary, worried, ageing. His plan of attack was a stale repetition of Blenheim and Ramillies – first attack the enemy flanks, then put in the decisive stroke against his centre. The Battle of Malplaquet on 11 September 1709 saw attack after attack rebound from the French defences with appalling loss. Only after between 16,000 and 18,000 soldiers, a fifth of the total engaged, had fallen did the French retreat, and then in good order. Even the oldest veterans were appalled by the carnage, which fell principally on the Dutch and least of all on the British, reserved by the Duke for the final assault.

Marlborough himself ran a high fever after the battle, sleepless, agonised by headaches, so shaken was he by what he termed 'a very murdering battle'. Even three weeks later he was confiding to Godolphin that 'the lamentable sight and thoughts of it have given me so much disquietude that I believe it is the chief cause of my illness; for it is melancholy to see so many brave men killed with whom I have lived these eight years, when we thought ourselves sure of a peace.'

The Battle of Malplaquet; engraving of 1736

The Duke nevertheless believed that Malplaquet would bring the French to accept the allied terms. He was mistaken: French morale had been raised by their army's gallant fight and the high allied losses, and peace lay further off than ever. Moreover Malplaquet also misled him in making a major false move in regard to his own career: he asked Anne to appoint him Captain-General for life. The request sprang from a reviving sense of personal insecurity. But the Queen turned him down; a fresh humiliation. Moreover his request played into the hands of his enemies, who alleged that he wished to make himself a military dictator like Cromwell.

On 18 November Marlborough returned to England for the winter. Now his career was running on into the shadows. The Queen, Harley and Abigail were ready to begin their long-meditated counter-attack on the Whigs and the Marlboroughs. The Queen indeed challenged the Duke's authority over the army itself by making military appointments behind his back – one of them Abigail's useless and drunken brother Jack. An

interview between Queen and Captain-General ended in the Duke for
once losing his temper and striding angrily from the room. 'Let me beg of
your majesty,' he wrote later, 'to reflect what your own people and the rest
of the world must think, who have been witnesses of the love, zeal and
duty with which I have served you, when they shall see that after all I have
done it has not been enough to protect me from the malice of a bedchamber woman.'

But at the urging of his friend Godolphin and the Whig leaders, he
deleted from the letter an ultimatum to the Queen to choose between
himself and Abigail. Again he displayed that curious dislike for standing
alone. It was fatal act of appeasement, which opened the way for the
Queen and Harley to pick off their enemies one by one.

'I have never, during this war, gone into the field,' wrote Marlborough
in spring 1710, 'with so heavy a heart as I do at this time.' Even the purely
official relationship between Queen Anne and Sarah, as head of the royal
household, now stood near breaking-point. As Lord Dartmouth, who was
then at Court, recorded:

The last free conference she had with her was at Windsor, where Mrs Danvers,
who was then in waiting, told me, the duchess reproached the queen for above an
hour with her own and her family's services, in so loud and shrill a voice that the
footmen at the bottom of the backstairs could hear her; and all this storm was
raised for the queen's having ordered a bottle of wine a day to be allowed for her
laundress, without her acquainting her grace with it. The queen, seeing her so
outrageous, got up, to have gone out of the room: the duchess clapped her back
against the door, and told her that she should hear her out, for that was the least
favour she could do her, in return for having set and kept the crown upon her
head. As soon as she had done raging, she flounced out of the room, and said, she
did not care if she never saw her more; to which the queen replied very calmly,
that she thought the seldomer the better.

In April 1710, at Kensington Palace, the two women met for the last
time. Sarah, once the most powerful woman in the kingdom after Anne
herself, waited in a window-seat in the gallery while the page went to see if
the Queen would see her, just like, in Sarah's own words, 'a Scotch lady
with a petition instead of a trusted and lifelong confidante'.

For Marlborough in the field, besieging and taking French fortresses in
succession, this was only the beginning of the year's bad news from home.
The Queen, prompted by Harley, dismissed her hated Whig ministers
one by one. It was not only malice and political rivalry; Harley correctly
perceived that the Whigs, the 'hawks', were out of touch with the nation,
which now wanted peace. Marlborough, feeling more and more friend-
less and isolated, wrote home: 'Am I not to be pitied that am every day in
danger of exposing my life for the good of those who are seeking my
ruin?' Without the Queen's trust and affection, the Duke no longer was

willing to take bold military risks in his earlier style. 'I now feel,' he told Godolphin, 'though I mean never so well, should I not have good success, I should find too many ready to blame me, so that if I am more cautious than heretofore, I hope the Queen will approve of it.'

In August came tidings that the Queen had dismissed Godolphin himself – and without even the kindness of a final interview. Harley was appointed Chancellor of the Exchequer and effectively her chief minister. But still the Duke did not resign.

When that December the Duke returned to his official residence in The Hague, the Mauritshuis, at the end of the campaigning season, he faced a grim personal dilemma. He was absolutely alone now: the Tories had won a General Election and Harley had been made Lord Treasurer. But Harley, via an intermediary, offered to make a deal: if Marlborough would publicly abandon the Whig side and induce Sarah to resign her court offices, the new government would support him in his post of Captain-General. Yet despite all Sarah's indiscretions and their catastrophic effect on his career, the Duke could not, would not, do other than stick by her. Their partnership against the world still held fast. As he wrote to her, 'My greatest concern is if possible to avoid the harsh usage which is most certainly resolved to be put in practice against you, for whom I must ever be more concerned than for all the other things in this world.'

When the Duke reluctantly at last returned to England in January 1711, people wondered to see him, in the words of an eyewitness, 'much thinner and greatly altered'. He went on his knees before the Queen in order to plead with her not to sack Sarah, or, at least, to extend the period of notice. But the Queen demanded the Gold Key – symbol of Sarah's office as Mistress of the Robes – within three days. Marlborough begged that at least it might be ten. The Queen changed her mind. She now demanded the key within *two* days.

In early summer 1711 the Duke took the field in what was to prove his last campaign. He had been bluntly told by Harley and his colleagues that he was merely a military subordinate now, owing strict obedience to their instructions. Yet he still soldiered on. Why did he not resign? Some historians have said that he wanted to cling on to his post – and the income – at all costs. He himself said that he stayed on out of public duty; out of loyalty to the allies. But his failure to resign in the face of the dismissal of his wife and colleagues and of personal humiliation may also be yet another example of that curious appeasing streak in his nature. It is one of the mysteries about Marlborough that although he was steel on the battlefield he was so often silk off it.

So he plunged back into the familiar military tasks – a vast correspondence arranging bread and other food supplies, forage, billets, contingents of mercenary troops. Here was another aspect of Marlborough's genius as a soldier – the ability to make things work in an age of general inefficiency. His army was always well fed and promptly paid; its marches superbly organised. This was more than the French absolute monarchy and its vaunted military system achieved.

Now, for all his troubles and his bitter feelings, he carried out perhaps the most brilliant offensive of his whole career. In fact, he himself was so proud of this 1711 campaign that he commemorated it with two tapestries in his new palace instead of the one allotted to each of his previous campaigns. His aim was to break through the *Ne Plus Ultra* Lines, a kind of eighteenth-century Maginot Line across northern France: redoubts, rivers and canals all linked together, inundations. He succeeded by means of subtle psychological deception – double bluffs, play-acting for the benefit of spies in his own camp. By these means he tricked the French command into believing that he was about to launch his grand attack in the western sector of the *Ne Plus Ultra* Lines, near Arras. But that night he force-marched his army eastwards. Before the French commander, Villars, could switch his own forces, the Duke slipped through the Lines by a causeway over inundations which he had tricked Villiars into leaving unguarded – and without losing a man. The way was open for him to lay siege to the fortress of Bouchain.

On 14 September 1711 Bouchain surrendered, and for the last time the Duke watched a defeated French garrison march out before him. In January 1712 the Queen finally dismissed him, on the pretext of trumped-up charges that he had pocketed public money. The Queen's letter was, in Sarah's words, 'so very offensive that the Duke threw it in the fire, though he was not a man of passion'. For Harley and his colleagues no longer needed him. Peace was on its way, negotiated with Louis XIV behind the backs of England's allies. But when the Treaty of Utrecht was signed in 1713, the Marlboroughs themselves were in self-imposed exile in Europe, enjoying the hospitality of rulers who still esteemed the Duke as the greatest European figure of the day.

The Peace Treaty secured the allies all they had really gone to war for – though less than they might have secured during the abortive negotiations of 1709. In particular Louis XIV accepted that France and Spain should never be united under a single monarchy, and recognised the Protestant succession to the English throne. The overweening power of royal France had been broken; ahead lay decline, bankruptcy and finally, in 1789, revolution. But England emerged from the war the world's most buoyant commercial power, the strongest seapower – launched on that rise to greatness which one day would make English the international language of the planet. The leadership of John Churchill, Duke of Marlborough, had decided the course of history.

On the death of Queen Anne in 1714, the Marlboroughs returned to England. The Duke was made Captain-General once more, restored to the post by the first official document signed by the new king, George I. In 1719 Blenheim Palace was far enough completed for the Duke and Sarah to go and live there at last. He was an old man now, crippled by a stroke. But before his death after another stroke in 1722 at the age of seventy-two, he enjoyed living quietly with his family . . . strolling on Sarah's arm round his new gardens and through his great house. War was now no more than a tapestry to embellish a palace. Once he paused before a portrait of himself in his prime by Sir Godfrey Kneller and remarked with sad wonder: 'That was once a man.'

South front of Blenheim Palace

LLOYD GEORGE

JOHN GRIGG

Disraeli wrote of the British people that 'being subject to fogs and possessing a powerful middle class' they required 'grave statesmen'. But he did not meet the requirement himself (as his biographer, Robert Blake, justly claims), and even less was it met by the next outsider to reach the British premiership, David Lloyd George.

Like Disraeli, Lloyd George sprang from an ethnic minority and made a virtue of his provenance. He too was humorous and detached in outlook, and not conditioned by the influence of Oxford or Cambridge. Both men were outraged by poverty and genuinely anxious to use the power of the State to combat social evils. But at the same time both were ambitious for themselves; Lloyd George would have agreed with Disraeli that he went into politics at least as much 'for fame' as for any other reason. Both in a sense were crooks, but crookedness was incidental to their main qualities and subservient to their higher purposes. They could, and often did, humbug others, but they were not self-deceivers. There the resemblance ends, but despite many differences they seem to have more in common with each other than with the rest of the British prime ministers.

David Lloyd George was born on 17 January 1863 – not in Wales, but in Manchester, where his father, William George, was at the time headmaster of a school. William George was a Pembrokeshire man who, like his famous son, spent most of his working life outside Wales. But it was while teaching at a school at Pwllheli in Caernarvonshire that he met and married Elizabeth Lloyd. They had three children – Mary, David and William – but the third was born posthumously, because in 1864 the father died, having retired in poor health to his native county. Elizabeth and the children then went to live with her brother, Richard, in the small village of Llanystumdwy, Caernarvonshire, on the road from Criccieth to Pwllheli.

Richard Lloyd – or 'Uncle Lloyd', as he became known to the George children – was a key figure in Lloyd George's life. As uncle and guardian, he early perceived the boy's extraordinary promise and devoted himself to nurturing it. By trade he was a master-cobbler, employing several men in the workshop attached to his cottage, where footwear was made and mended for the whole neighbourhood. But he was also a local sage – a master-cobbler of the Hans Sachs type. His grandfather had been prominent in the cultural life of North Wales, and Uncle Lloyd was immersed in it too. He was, moreover, unpaid local minister of the Baptist sect known as Campbellites, or Disciples of Christ, and his sermons were much admired. In the later Victorian period Wales was experiencing a national revival. Nonconformist chapels, old and new, were resounding to the eloquence of great Welsh preachers and to the compulsive sound of great Welsh hymns; while together with the religious fervour went a new

*Richard Lloyd ('Uncle Lloyd')
with his nephew at 11 Downing
Street during the latter's
Chancellorship of the Exchequer*

political self-awareness and a new pride in Welsh language and literature. Uncle Lloyd was the sort of man to be in the forefront of this national advance.

His relative poverty (and one must stress that it was only relative, because in Llanystumdwy he was one of the most prosperous citizens) was unimportant compared with the fact that he belonged, and was recognised as belonging, to the Welsh cultural élite of his day. Indeed, his simple life was a reproach and a challenge to the anglicised squirearchy and Anglican church establishment which were then the chief butts of Welsh nationalism. The George children were certainly not brought up to feel that they were underdogs. On the contrary, they were brought up in the knowledge that they *mattered* in their own community, and that it was their duty to show how much Wales mattered in the wider British community. David, in particular, was encouraged from his earliest years to believe that he had a special historic destiny, and the belief came to him naturally enough.

His only formal education was at the village school, which was run by the Established Church, anathema to all good Nonconformists. But he acquired an excellent grounding there and later acknowledged his debt to the headmaster, David Evans. He was good at mathematics and once told his elder son that he first became aware that he was a genius while reading Euclid in the top branches of an oak-tree. He was also given assistance in his studies by Uncle Lloyd. But above all he taught *himself* by extensive and very methodical reading. Beyond a certain point Uncle Lloyd could not help him in English, because his own English was poor. But Elizabeth had brought her husband's books with her from Pembrokeshire, and they were invaluable to David and his younger brother, William. They included Shakespeare's plays, Green's *History of England*, Burnet's *History of the Reformation*, Hallam's *Constitutional History* and much else. David had a marvellous memory, which he supplemented by taking detailed notes. For instance, he wrote a chapter-by-chapter précis of Green's *History*. Macaulay's essays were great favourites, and he also read novels, particularly Dickens and Victor Hugo's *Les Misérables*, which he read in a cheap translation and by which he was considerably influenced. (He once said that the test of a good book was that it should be 'at least fifty years old and sold at sixpence in any decent bookseller's shop'.) Though never scholarly, he was far better read than most politicians educated at public schools, and his vivid imagination enabled him to benefit fully from everything that he read.

On the whole Lloyd George found his childhood at Llanystumdwy very tedious, but he loved the surrounding country and more especially the river that flows through the village – the Dwyfor – which he made part of his title when, at the very end of his life, he was persuaded to accept an earldom. He had a punishing dose of organised religion, involving three chapel services every Sunday, and when he was twelve his uncle baptised him in the brook beside the Campbellite chapel on the outskirts of Criccieth. But he used to say that the following night he had a sort of negative revelation, in which he suddenly realised that he did not at all believe what he had been taught to believe. Certainly, his astonishing independence of mind enabled him to escape, long before he was grown-up, from the cultural and religious orthodoxy of his home environment. He largely rejected puritanism, and would have agreed with Julian Grenfell that life was 'colour and warmth and light, and a striving evermore for these'. He believed in hard work and was disgusted by drunkenness, but in other respects we search him in vain for traces of the Nonconformist conscience. He was bored to tears by chapel services, apart from good sermons and hymns which he always enjoyed. Moreover the supernatural element in religion was not for him. His idea of Christianity was that it was a religion of social progress rather than one of personal salvation.

After leaving school, and after passing the necessary law examination, he became an articled clerk with a firm of solicitors at Portmadoc, about nine miles from Llanystumdwy. Portmadoc was then a flourishing port and shipyard, full of sailing ships which carried slate from the quarries of Blaenau Ffestiniog to ports of northern Europe such as Bremen and Hamburg, or brought cargoes of dried cod from as far away as New-foundland. Lloyd George loved to talk to their captains and crews about the distant places they visited. What they told him did something to satisfy his curiosity, while at the same time increasing his *Wanderlust*. At Portmadoc he also became a star performer in the local debating society and wrote articles on general politics for the local press. Soon he struck out on his own as an independent solicitor, and in due course was joined by his younger brother, William, who in the years ahead did most of the donkey-work and so enabled the firm to finance David during his early years in Parliament.

There was never any question of his being content to remain a pro-vincial attorney or even a provincial politician. From the very first he meant to go to the top. One of his cases as a solicitor established his reputation as a champion of the Welsh national cause. This was the Llanfrothen burial case in 1888, which he won in the High Court, and which made him a household name in Wales. Two years later he was elected to the House of Commons, at a by-election, for the Caernarvon Boroughs constituency, which he represented without interruption for well over half a century. At the time of his election he was only twenty-seven.

Two years before his election to Parliament Lloyd George was married to Margaret Owen. She was the only daughter of a prosperous tenant farmer living on high ground overlooking Criccieth. The courtship was not all plain sailing. The Owens were Methodists, to whom Disciples of Christ seemed a relatively low form of Nonconformist life. Moreover, they had doubts about Lloyd George's character and prospects, and Margaret herself – though immensely attracted by him – was disturbed by what she heard of his easy way with women. Eventually his persistence overcame all obstacles; they were married in 1888 and their first child was born the following year.

Margaret had been sent away to school and was better educated than her parents. She was adored by them, as Lloyd George was by his family. In a sense, therefore, they were both spoiled children, and this con-tributed to the tension and conflict which marred, but never destroyed, their marriage. Both were brought up to feel that the world was their oyster, but the world that mattered to her was North Wales, whereas the world that mattered to him was – the world. His attachment to Wales was more spiritual than physical. He loved the Welsh language and cultural

Portmadoc at the end of the 19th century

tradition, and also rejoiced in the company of Welsh people. But he detested the Welsh climate and was naturally drawn to countries where as a rule the sun shone, the landscape glowed and the sea sparkled. Margaret, on the other hand, would have been well content to spend all her life in her native country and did, in fact, spend most of her time there during his early years as an MP.

Beyond question it was dangerous to leave a man of his temperament on his own in London. He needed constant female attention, not only to satisfy his very strong amorous impulses but also because he liked his creature comforts and was never any good at looking after himself. Apart from casual flirtations, he had at least one quite steady and semi-serious affair as a young MP with the wife of Timothy Evans, an enterprising Welsh draper in London, who accepted the situation philosophically. Margaret became very jealous and there were bitter recriminations until, at length, she decided to spend more time with her husband, and to acquire a London home for the family. But one must not exaggerate the womanising side of Lloyd George, which has made him something of a cult figure in the age of permissiveness. His dominating passion was always politics, not sex.

The Lloyd Georges had five children – Richard, Mair, Olwen, Gwilym and Megan. All were born at Criccieth, because Margaret trusted her local doctor and would have dreaded to have a confinement anywhere else. Though later on bad terms with his elder son, Lloyd George was quite a good father, as great men go, and the children loved to have him around.

Lloyd George with his first wife and daughters Mair and Megan, c.1904

He would tell them stories from the classics, using his gift of mimicry to impersonate the characters. For all his egocentricity, he was devoted to them and took a genuine interest in their lives. They were certainly afraid of him, but not because he was unduly severe or cowed them with the threat of corporal punishment. In 1907 – just before he became Chancellor of the Exchequer – Mair died from a mismanaged attack of appendicitis, and Lloyd George was for a short time prostrated. It was the worst personal affliction he ever suffered, but his extraordinary buoyancy of spirit enabled him to recover swiftly.

When he took his seat at Westminster in 1890 he did so, ostensibly, as a follower of Gladstone, though in fact he derived more inspiration from Joseph Chamberlain and was a Gladstonian only because Wales was blindly loyal to the GOM. Arriving after a by-election he was momentarily in the limelight on the day he took his seat. But soon the limelight became a normal condition of life for him, because he quickly established himself as a very effective back-bench Parliamentarian. His maiden speech got him off to a good start. Most new Members jump in, as it were, at the shallow end, with maiden speeches containing nothing but innocuous platitudes. But Lloyd George plunged in at the deep end with a sarcastic attack on two Parliamentary giants (whom he secretly much admired), Joseph Chamberlain and Lord Randolph Churchill – rather as Aneurin Bevan did nearly forty years later, when the two statesmen attacked were Winston Churchill and Lloyd George himself. His brashness might have turned the House against him, but in fact it worked the other way. MPs soon got into the habit of listening to him, even when they disliked what he was saying. He was also soon much in demand as a platform speaker throughout the country.

His speeches were so well delivered that they sounded spontaneous, even though he took immense trouble in preparing them and usually learned them by heart. During his first nine years in Parliament he made his name as a debater and became the unofficial leader of the Welsh group of MPs. Most of his energy was devoted to Welsh causes, such as tithe, land rating, disestablishment and (limited) home rule. But he also came to be regarded as an outstanding spokesman for Nonconformity in general, and for the radical school of Liberalism. On the whole he steered clear of foreign affairs, though in 1898 he showed astonishing originality in denouncing anti-French jingoism during the Fashoda crisis, when most leading politicians, Liberal as well as Tory, were prepared to go to war with France.

In any case he was far from insular in his personal habits. Beginning early, and despite restricted means, to indulge his lifelong taste for travel, he went abroad as often as possible when Parliament was in recess, more especially in winter. He loved the South of France and other parts of the Mediterranean seaboard, but he also went further afield, travelling to Argentina in 1896 and to Canada in 1899. By the turn of the century he was already exceptional among British politicians of the period for the number of foreign countries he had visited, though he never mastered any foreign language – apart from English.

He was at Vancouver, in the far west of Canada, when news reached him of impending conflict in South Africa, and he immediately sent a message home protesting against the 'outrage . . . perpetrated in the name of freedom'. His opposition to the Boer war, which nearly cost him his life, but in the end established him as a national figure, sprang from neither pacifism nor Little Englandism, but from a rational conviction that this particular war was mistaken, as well as from a moral conviction that it was unjust. He was never, in fact, a pacifist, and far from being hostile to the British Empire believed in it strongly. But his form of imperialism was different from Chamberlain's. He resented English arrogance towards other races (particularly white races) and thought that the Empire, like the United Kingdom, should be based upon the principle of 'home rule all round'. In this he anticipated what he later went some way towards realising, the British Commonwealth of Nations.

At the time, however, his views were odious to the majority of his compatriots, including many in Wales. Tories regarded him as a traitor, and a section of his Liberal colleagues repudiated him, because they supported the war. But through all the military ups and downs he never wavered in his opinion. At the outset he predicted to a friend that the war would cost the country 10,000 men and £50 million, which seemed preposterous but was, in fact, a very substantial under-estimate. The eventual cost was 22,000 men and £250 million.

On 18 December 1901 he kept a speaking engagement in Birmingham, despite grave warnings from the police and others that he was risking his life by venturing into the heart of Chamberlain's political territory. The meeting was in Birmingham Town Hall, where a year before Elgar's *Dream of Gerontius* had received its first performance. Lloyd George had to face a very different sort of music. Outside there was a crowd of 30,000, and the Hall itself was packed with about 7000, many of whom were gate-crashers. As they waited for Lloyd George they waved Union Jacks and chanted patriotic songs. It was providential that he ever managed to get into the building, and even more providential that he emerged from it alive. When he rose to speak the platform was pelted with missiles, while the crowd outside hurled bricks and stones through the windows. Lloyd George could not make himself heard and was eventually persuaded by the Chief Constable to leave the stage. As the wounded were attended to

Lloyd George in 1903

in the basement he was smuggled out of the building amid a detachment of police, disguised as one of them. But the riot went on for a considerable time, until the crowd was at last dispersed by the combined effects of a truncheon charge and a snowstorm. Many people were injured and two were killed, including one policeman.

The Birmingham drama established him once and for all in the popular imagination. Moreover, as the war dragged to its close, enthusiasm for it waned, and many who had execrated him began to feel that he might not be so far wrong after all. Within the Liberal Party his star was in the ascendant, because most Liberals broadly shared his view – among them the leader, Sir Henry Campbell-Bannerman. Between 1902 and 1905 he came to be regarded as a likely member of the next Liberal Cabinet, and his somewhat hypocritical campaign against Balfour's 1902 Education Act, as well as his more genuine attacks on Chamberlain's Tariff Reform proposals, further enhanced his reputation. When Campbell-

An artist's impression of the Birmingham Town Hall riot of 18 December 1901

Bannerman formed his government at the end of 1905 the only question was not whether Lloyd George would receive a Cabinet post, but which. In fact, he was appointed President of the Board of Trade, and over the next two and a half years proved himself a resourceful and conciliatory minister. His record of legislation was impressive and, when Asquith succeeded to the Premiership in 1908, it was no surprise that Lloyd George succeeded him as Chancellor of the Exchequer.

He arrived at the Treasury at a time of slackening impetus for the Government and renewed hope for the Opposition. A trade recession had set in and it seemed that Chamberlain's protectionist doctrine might be right after all. Tariff Reform gave the Tories (whose ally Chamberlain had originally become on the Irish Home Rule issue) a radical appeal to complement their appeal to traditional interests. Lloyd George decided at once to use his position to enable the Liberals to make a fighting comeback. His chief instrument was to be the Budget, but in 1908 the Budget had already been prepared by Asquith and was introduced by him after he became Prime Minister. Lloyd George saw the Finance Bill through and implemented the proposal for old age pensions, a reform in which he had long believed. Then he turned his mind to his own Budget for the following year.

This was the most important and controversial in British history. Before preparing it he visited Germany to study the Bismarckian scheme of social insurance and labour exchanges, because he was determined to make a deliberate attack upon poverty and unemployment in Britain. Lloyd George had always been a social reformer. Even before his election to Parliament he told a Welsh audience: 'There is a momentous time coming. The dark continent of wrong is being explored, and there is a missionary spirit abroad for its reclamation to the realm of right. A holy war has been proclaimed against "man's inhumanity to man", and the people of Europe are thronging to the crusade.' But he was always a pragmatist rather than a theorist, and it was only when he became Chancellor of the Exchequer, with the power to give effect to his aspirations, that he began to study the general British social problem in detail. In doing so he worked closely with Charles Masterman and others of the new school of Liberalism, who reacted against Gladstonian *laissez-faire* and believed that the State should assume more responsibility for the welfare of the people. He also worked closely with Winston Churchill, a recent convert to Liberalism and his successor at the Board of Trade, who was his admitted disciple and with whom he maintained an uneasy friendship over the years.

The 1909 Budget recaptured the initiative for the Liberal Party. Designed to finance a big programme of social reform and national development, it tapped new sources of revenue, of which by far the most significant, in the long run, was the super-tax on large incomes. It also outraged the landed interest by calling for a valuation of land and imposing land taxes (though in the event these proved to be of small consequence). The Opposition denounced the Budget with a fury that was at least partly synthetic. Chamberlain – old and crippled by a stroke – wanted to defeat Lloyd George's radical programme because it was a rival to his own, and Balfour, the Tory leader, was above all determined to bring the Government down. They did not scruple to use the House of Lords to precipitate a general election, but by resorting to such an antique and anti-democratic weapon they played into Lloyd George's hands.

In a succession of brilliant speeches, before and after the Lords – disregarding long-established custom – rejected his Finance Bill, he heaped obloquy upon the Second Chamber and all that it symbolised. His oratory combined the imagery and moral fervour of Welsh preaching with the wit and sarcasm of Disraeli or Randolph Churchill and a humorous fancy that was all his own. At Newcastle, for instance, he said on 9 October 1909:

Let them realise what they are doing. They are forcing a revolution, and they will get it. The Lords may decree a revolution, but the people will direct it. If they begin, issues will be raised that they little dream of. Questions will be asked which are now whispered in humble voices, and answers will be demanded then with authority. The question will be asked whether five hundred men, ordinary men chosen accidentally from among the unemployed, should override the judgment – the deliberate judgment – of millions of people who are engaged in the industry which makes the wealth of the country.

To refer to the peers as *ordinary* men chosen *accidentally* from among the *unemployed* was a masterstroke. Deference was still very strong in Britain, and people were still disposed to take the House of Lords as seriously as it took itself. But by an inspired choice of words Lloyd George cut it down to size.

Was he, as his opponents alleged, an apostle of class war? Certainly he had a rooted antipathy to landlords (in both senses, but particularly in the sense of landowners). He saw nothing good in the English feudal hangover and even as a boy recorded in his diary the view that land should be tenable only for a single lifetime – that it should be redistributed with each generation. As a practical politician he later modified this view, but he always disliked stately homes and what they stood for. On the other hand he approved of the self-made rich and tended to like them personally. Moreover, he was able to get on with many aristocrats and country gentlemen as individuals, while attacking them as a class. His policy, he said, was to fire at the line of battle rather than at individual soldiers in it.

In any case he was definitely not, in the accepted modern sense, a

BUDGET.—" Did you say that you wouldn't swallow me without mincing ? "
LORD LANSDOWNE.—" No, sir—please, sir—I never said *mincing*, I might have said *wincing*."
(*By permission of " The Westminster Gazette*.")

A cartoonist's view of the 1909 Budget

socialist. Indeed, his reforms were partly designed to meet the challenge of the fledgeling Labour Party, in which socialist ideas were already strong. His aim was to pay for social welfare by a combination of insurance and growing tax revenue. In January 1910 the Liberals just won the election which was fought specifically on the Budget and which ensured its passage. The fact that their victory was so narrow – leaving them dependent upon the Irish Nationalists – was due above all to the appeal of Tariff Reform as an alternative radical programme for the country, and to the preponderant bourgeois bias in the electorate (which still comprised only sixty per cent of adult males, and of course no women).

At the end of 1910 there was a second general election to decide whether or not the Lords' power to delay legislation should be limited, and their power to hold up 'money bills' removed. The Liberals again won, by much the same margin, and in 1911 the Parliament Act was passed. This formally curbed the Lords' powers, but was nevertheless a

Lloyd George with pet pug

botched measure, because the composition of the House was left unchanged. To the extent that it has since shown restraint it has done so far more because of the fear of being abolished – which would have existed anyway – than because of the Parliament Act.

1911 also saw the passage of Lloyd George's National Health Insurance scheme, which has been described by the best student of it (the American historian, Professor Bentley B. Gilbert) as a 'stupendous' achievement, taking the State 'into an entirely new field of activity'. But for Lloyd George it would never have been conceived in the form it was, and certainly it would never have been carried in the teeth of dogged resistance from vested interests, particularly the doctors. Many socialists disliked the insurance principle, which made the measure acceptable to Liberal capitalists, but Lloyd George persuaded most Labour MPs to vote for it in return for a promise – which he was glad enough to give, on the merits of the case – that the innovation of payment of Members would be introduced.

Between 1911 and the outbreak of war in 1914 the Liberal Government had to deal with mounting social unrest. There was trade union militancy on an unprecedented scale, the suffragettes were on the rampage, and

Ulster Unionist resistance to Home Rule – which the Government had to promote, because of its dependence upon the Irish nationalists – threatened the country with civil war. Lloyd George did his best to conciliate labour, and was undoubtedly the Liberals' most popular figure in working-class eyes. He was keen to obtain votes for women, having always believed in woman's suffrage, but he wanted the reform to come as part of a general democratisation of the franchise. He was prepared to compromise on Ireland, having never acknowledged the exclusive case for Irish Home Rule and being aware, as most Liberals were not, of the force of Protestant Ulster's objections to it. Above all, he was conscious of the danger of national disunity when the German challenge to British power was assuming ever more alarming proportions. During the struggle over the House of Lords he had actually proposed, secretly, that there should be a coalition government to settle contentious issues on a reciprocal basis. But the proposal came to nothing, though it appealed to some of the leaders on both sides.

In 1912 he fell in love with a woman twenty-five years younger than himself, who was to become his mistress and eventually – after Margaret's death – his wife. Frances Stevenson was of mixed Scottish, French and Italian extraction, and she first entered the Lloyd George family circle as holiday governess to his daughter Megan. She was a career girl with ideas of female emancipation (she had not read Wells's *Ann Veronica* for nothing), but also with a strongly conventional side. She was valuable to Lloyd George because she ministered to him with slavish devotion, not least as a confidential secretary. Later on she had another lover, but she was indulgent towards Lloyd George's own frequent lapses and there was never any question of her leaving him, despite the invidious position she was in. He made it clear at the outset that he would not marry her at the price of being divorced from Margaret, because that would ruin his career. But the truth was that he did not want to be parted from Margaret in any case. Both women were necessary to him and for about thirty years he was, in effect, a bigamist.

The cataclysm which occurred in 1914 transformed him from a great peace minister into a great war minister. The switch was painful and difficult for him, but once he had made up his mind there was no turning back, and all his energy and talent were devoted to the war effort. The thing that decided him was the German invasion of Belgium, because he hated to see a small nation (like the Boers, earlier) trampled down by a large empire. But he had always been a firm believer in British sea power and saw Germany as a threat to it. He had astonished Europe by the forthrightness of his warning to Germany at the time of the Agadir crisis in 1911. He also loved France and had long maintained that Britain and

An early picture of Frances Stevenson

France must stand together as the only important democracies in Europe. His decision to back the war permanently estranged him from the pacifist wing of the Liberal Party (which had misunderstood his attitude towards the Boer war) but made many Tories see him in a new light. From having been an intensely controversial, not to say hated, figure, he became a nationally accepted champion of Britain's cause.

His first major service to it was to avert a financial crash when war broke out. By proclaiming four consecutive Bank Holidays he gave himself a breathing-space during which, among other things, he introduced a paper currency to take the place of the old gold coinage. The City's gratitude to him was fervent – and significant, in view of its former hostility. He soon grasped the novel character of the war and looked for ways of building an effective front in the Balkans to help break the deadlock on the Western Front.

In May 1915, when the British Army was in danger of early collapse through shortage of warlike equipment, he agreed to step down from the Exchequer to take the entirely new post of Minister of Munitions. Starting from a single office room with two secretaries, two tables and one chair, he rapidly improvised an organisation which delivered the goods on a spectacular scale. As the Army expanded far beyond the wildest calculations of 1914, so he provided arms and ammunition in the quantities that the Army needed. He also wrenched the responsibility for design and development away from the War Office, and as a result such novelties as the Stokes mortar and the tank saw the light of day.

His methods were highly unconventional, indeed revolutionary. Instead of having arms manufactured by just the Service establishments, such as Woolwich Arsenal, plus a few outside firms, he brought 4000 firms into the business in one way or another, and saw that they were under his Ministry's general control. Moreover, he appointed businessmen rather than civil servants or technical experts to many key posts in the Ministry. What he wanted, and what on the whole he got, were 'men of push and go'.

His tremendous impact upon British industry was not only vital for winning the war. It also had historic side-effects, such as the opportunity given to women to prove that they could do all sorts of jobs which formerly only men were thought capable of doing. This led naturally to the franchise for women in 1918. As Minister of Munitions he was also able to do much to improve conditions of work in factories. The exceptional powers he possessed gave him new scope for social reform. From the first he did his best to carry the trade unions with him, though on Christmas Day 1915 he was shouted down by Clydeside workers at a meeting in St Andrew's Hall, Glasgow – an incident full of menace for the future.

After his triumphant stint at the Ministry of Munitions Lloyd George was for a few months Secretary of State for War before, in December 1916, succeeding Asquith as Prime Minister. Asquith himself and many other Liberals felt that he had contrived to get the job by devious and disloyal means, but they did him less than justice. He only wanted a more efficient direction of the war and would have been content for Asquith to retain the Premiership if he (Lloyd George) had been free to run the war. But the breach with Asquith had disastrous consequences for the Liberal Party, and was also bad for Lloyd George, because it deprived him of his party base and left him more or less on his own, temporarily indispensable but in due course expendable. No leading Liberal joined his Coalition, which from the first rested largely upon Conservative support.

Yet nobody could doubt that it was, in the fullest sense, his government – and what a remarkable one it was, breaking all sorts of new ground. New departments were brought into being, such as Labour, Transport, Housing and Pensions. For the first time the Cabinet was given a secretariat and minutes were kept of its meetings. Completely new people were brought into government from outside politics, such as an eminent historian and university vice-chancellor, H. A. L. Fisher, to be Minister of Education, and a number of businessmen to occupy key posts, one of whom, Sir Joseph Maclay, put in charge of Shipping, did not even become a member of either House of Parliament. This was an unheard-of breach of the constitutional rules, and in 1917 General J. C. Smuts, who had fought against us in the Boer war, became a member of the War Cabinet, again without being a member of the British Parliament. Finally, Lloyd George formed a small but high-powered secretariat of his own, which became known as the 'Garden Suburb', because huts to accommodate it were erected in the garden of 10 Downing Street. This enabled him to by-pass the established hierarchies of Whitehall – a practice which naturally caused a good deal of resentment, but which also enabled him to exercise more control over the whole machine of government than had ever before been exercised by a Prime Minister.

Did he 'win the war'? Apart from all that he had done before reaching the Premiership, he undoubtedly put new life into the British war effort after the ghastly frustration of the Somme in 1916. Without a man of his resourcefulness and buoyancy it is unlikely that the country would have weathered the last stages of the storm. More specifically, he had much to do with the Admiralty's reluctant conversion to the convoy system, which narrowly averted defeat by the U-boats. On the other hand, he failed to avert further appalling carnage on the Western Front, partly because he grossly overrated the French general, Nivelle, and partly because even he did not feel quite strong enough to dismiss Haig, whose military talents he certainly did not overrate. But when the Germans launched their last big offensive in the spring of 1918, he kept his nerve and used the crisis to obtain a unified Allied command in the West. Those who worked closely with him and those who only saw him from afar were alike ready to testify that it was he who sustained their morale in desperate times.

The general election which followed the Armistice at the end of 1918 returned his Coalition with an overwhelming majority. But in fact it was mainly a Conservative majority, which supported him as Prime Minister because his prestige was unequalled. It is very arguable that if anyone else had been leading the nation in the immediate post-war period there would have been a revolution. True, he created huge problems by prematurely scrapping wartime controls, but at the time any Conservative Prime Minister would have done the same. It is less likely, though, that a Conservative Prime Minister would have handled trade union leaders as skilfully and flexibly as he did, or would have extended unemployment benefit to cover twelve million workers. The Russian revolution was in everybody's mind and to some it was a challenge to act. A. J. P. Taylor has written that it was 'thanks to Lloyd George' that 'barricades were not set up in English streets'.

But his first task after the election was to lead the British delegation to the Peace Conference in Paris, which lasted from January to June 1919. He did some of the best work of his life at the Conference, but the circumstances could hardly have been more difficult, and he had to deal with some exceptionally difficult people. President Woodrow Wilson of the United States was self-righteous and opinionated, largely ignorant of European conditions, and increasingly out of touch with public opinion at home. Georges Clémenceau, the French Prime Minister, was a cantankerous, though formidable, old man, driven by the understandable strength of French feelings to take an even harder line about Germany than he might have wished to do if he had been a completely free agent.

Lloyd George himself had made some concessions to the prevailing Germanophobia in the course of the election campaign, but his true intentions were moderate and reasonable. The so-called 'Fontainebleau Memorandum' of 25 March 1919 is the fullest statement of his views at the time, and one which does him, on the whole, great credit. But he too was not a free agent. When it became known that he was trying to obtain tolerable terms for Germany, he was bitterly attacked by the Northcliffe Press and subjected to considerable pressure from Unionist backbenchers. All the same, he routed his critics in Parliament and persisted with his efforts in Paris. Inevitably he failed on many counts, but he also had his successes, and it is fair to say that without his skilful and determined brokerage the Treaty of Versailles would have been much worse than it was; indeed it might never in the end have been signed at all.

After its signature on 28 June he returned to London in triumph and was met at Victoria Station by King George V in person, accompanied by the young Prince of Wales. This moment was perhaps the supreme pinnacle of his career.

At home, though violence was averted in Great Britain, there was plenty of it in Ireland, but one of Lloyd George's greatest post-war achievements was to settle the Irish Question, so far as Britain was concerned, for fifty years. His settlement consisted of virtual independence for twenty-six Irish counties, while six remained with local self-government as part of the United Kingdom. It was an almost miraculous feat to get both the Republican terrorist, Michael Collins, and Tory politicians who in the past had adamantly opposed any Home Rule for Ireland, to agree to the compromise Treaty of 1921. He chose the right moment to negotiate, when the terrorists were pretty well beaten by the security forces, but at the same time British opinion was outraged by the methods used in fighting them. Even so, the odds were against agreement, because the Irish negotiators knew that they would split the Republican movement by signing the Treaty – 'signing their death warrant', as Collins put it. But somehow Lloyd George got them to sign, and so transformed an Anglo-Irish war into an Irish civil war, in which the IRA was temporarily crushed by the Irish themselves.

At one point in the Irish crisis he held a cabinet meeting in the council chamber of the Town Hall at Inverness. He was staying in the Highlands and feeling rather out of sorts, so he made the Cabinet come to him instead of returning to London as custom required. The King was staying nearby and gave him breakfast before the meeting, which (according to Tom Jones, assistant secretary to the Cabinet) was a great success. 'The weather was perfect, the town was highly flattered, the Provost important, the P.M. beaming, and even the Ministers who had scowled and growled at Euston melted into friendliness when they saw how delighted the Highlanders were to have them in their midst.' The whole thing was typical of Lloyd George's way of doing business – imaginative and unorthodox. He seemed immensely confident, with a power more akin to that of an American President than that of a British Prime Minister. Yet there was only a little more than a year to go before he was brought down.

One reason alleged for his downfall is that he prostituted his office by selling honours. It may have been a contributory factor, but too much should not be made of it. Honours have always been sold. The only difference, in Lloyd George's case, was that towards the end of his Premiership he abused the system more flagrantly than it is normally considered proper to abuse it. Though never scrupulous about money, he must not be seen as a common-or-garden crook. His motive was never to make money for its own sake, but rather to have the complete political independence that only private capital could give him. As a young MP, unpaid and without the personal wealth that most MPs then had, he got involved in a somewhat shady speculation in Patagonian gold shares. (Hence his trip to the Argentine in 1896.) When he was Chancellor of the Exchequer his career was nearly brought to an end, in 1912, by the Marconi affair, in which his role was reprehensible rather than scandalous, and from which, in any case, he did not derive any material gain.

But the honours business was more serious, because the Coalition Liberal share of the swag fell under his personal control. His view of the general ethics of the matter was pithily, though privately, explained to the Conservative, J. C. C. Davidson:

You and I know [selling honours] is a far cleaner method of filling the Party chest than the methods used in the United States or the Socialist Party. In America the steel trusts support one political party, and the cotton people support another. This places political parties under the domination of great financial interests and trusts. Here a man gives £40,000 to the Party and gets a baronetcy. If he comes to the Leader of the Party and says I subscribe largely to the Party funds, you must do this or that, we can tell him to go to the devil.

In fact the so-called Lloyd George fund, which he was later able to use to finance his political activities, was of complex origin and did not, as was whispered, consist simply of the proceeds of honours sales. Moreover, after his fall from power, he was able to sustain a high personal standard of living through his own legitimate earnings as journalist and author. The taint of corruption undoubtedly stuck to him, but there was hypocrisy as well as exaggeration in the charge, because his political enemies tended to fear his virtues far more than they disliked or disapproved of his faults.

The immediate cause of his downfall was that his foreign policy came unstuck. Since the Treaty of Versailles he had been working hard to bring about a general European settlement, with Germany and Soviet Russia re-integrated. But his efforts, though laudable, were in vain, and they distracted him from problems at home which needed his full attention. He had talked of making Britain 'a fit country for heroes to live in', but the reality mocked the phrase. Finally, he was led by an obsession about the Middle East into a confrontation with the new Turkey, led by Kemal Atatürk, which nearly landed Britain in another war. The Coalition was losing public support and the Conservative Party felt that the moment had come to smash it. But it was Tory back-benchers, not Lloyd George's principal Tory colleagues, who revolted and brought the Government to an end at the famous Carlton Club meeting in October 1922. Lloyd

George resigned as soon as he heard the result of the meeting. He needed a rest, having been in high office for seventeen continuous years. It did not occur to him that he would never hold office again.

He was destined to spend the rest of his life in the wilderness, during the 1920s still with a big organised following, during the 1930s increasingly isolated, though always a VIP, always drawing large crowds. The Labour Party was scarcely less hostile to him than the Conservatives, even though he was sympathetic to the strikers in the 1926 General Strike. He gathered around him some of the best minds in the country, including Keynes, and worked out plans for regenerating industry and agriculture, and for tackling the evil of mass unemployment. In the economic crisis of 1931 he would have had to be included in the National Government – as leader of the Liberal Party – if he had not been struck down at that very moment by a prostate operation. This was his last chance of a comeback in peacetime and it was tragic – for the country as well as for him – that it eluded him. Thereafter he was still treated almost as royalty as he went about the country, but in the harsh arithmetic of politics he counted for virtually nothing.

Unlike Sir Oswald Mosley he did not stray from the Parliamentary system, whose victim in a sense he was. He did not take to the streets. But was he ever attracted by fascism? Certainly he was attracted by Hitler, whom he visited in 1936. What particularly struck him was that Hitler had conquered unemployment in Germany, as he wished to conquer it in Britain. He also had an unnecessarily bad conscience about the Treaty of Versailles, which made him vulnerable to one aspect of Hitlerian propaganda. Yet he never ceased, himself, to be a staunch democrat, and was neither an appeaser nor – when the second War came – a defeatist. He believed in dealing with foreigners from a position of strength, and while he saw no way (before December 1941) of ending the war otherwise than by negotiation with Hitler, he maintained that we should negotiate only when we had shown quite clearly that we could not be defeated. If Hitler had not declared war on the United States after Pearl Harbor, it is more than likely that Lloyd George's analysis would have been proved right. His mistake was to ascribe to Hitler a normal degree of rationality.

Much of the last two decades or so of his life was spent at the house he had built for himself at Churt in Surrey – a sort of Colombey-les-deux-Eglises from which, however, he never returned. He wrote six volumes of war memoirs at prodigious speed, and he also became a successful fruit farmer. As his hopes of regaining power gradually faded his appearances in the House of Commons became more and more intermittent, though he could still make devastating speeches there on occasion. In June 1936, when the Baldwin government lifted the sanc-

Lloyd George with Hitler at Berchtesgaden

tions that it had imposed on Italy for invading Abyssinia, he delivered an attack which Churchill described as one of the greatest Parliamentary performances of all time. Baldwin had recently said, 'Let your aim be resolute and your footsteps firm and certain.' Lloyd George replied:

Here is the resolute aim; here is the certain footstep – running away . . . Only a few weeks after the election was over, [the Government was] negotiating treachery . . . Fifty nations ranged themselves behind that torch. They said, "Here is the British Prime Minister, with the greatest Empire in the world marching; we will range ourselves behind him". The Abyssinians believed it; the vast majority of the people of this country believed it. The Government had not been in for more than a few weeks before that torch was dimmed. Tonight it is quenched – with a hiss; a hiss that will be re-echoed throughout the whole world.

Harold Macmillan, who was present as a Tory back-bencher, has written of the speech: 'Nobody who heard it can ever forget the extraordinary power and scorn, enhanced by the Welsh intonation into which he always fell in moments of excitement, of the word "hiss".'

In the debate on the Norwegian campaign, in April 1940, Lloyd George made his last, though by no means least effective, intervention in the House of Commons. Neville Chamberlain – whom he had long disliked and despised – imprudently appealed for sacrifice, which gave Lloyd George the opportunity to say:

The orator in action: Lloyd George addresses the National Conference of the Liberal Free Trade Campaign in 1931

The nation is prepared for every sacrifice, so long as it has leadership . . . I say solemnly that the Prime Minister should give an example of sacrifice, because there is nothing that can contribute more to victory in this war than that he should sacrifice the seals of office.

Chamberlain did, in fact, resign as a result of obtaining too low a majority at the end of the debate, and of then failing to persuade Labour to join him in a Coalition. Churchill became Prime Minister and Lloyd George was rather hurt when his old disciple at first did not offer him a place in the War Cabinet – all the more so as Neville Chamberlain remained a member of it. But when, in due course, offers were made, Lloyd George refused them. He would not join the Cabinet, nor would he agree to go to Washington as Ambassador. He was no longer up to such work and knew, in his heart, that his career was over.

Margaret died at Criccieth in January 1941, but he was prevented by snow drifts from reaching her before she died. Already he was afflicted, though he did not know it, with the cancer that was to cause his own death. In the autumn of 1943 he married Frances Stevenson, and a year later moved with her to a farmhouse in his childhood village of Llanystumdwy. His father had returned to Wales to die, and he was doing the same. The

Dwyfor was only a short distance from the house, and he chose a spot beside it where he wished to be buried. On one walk he pointed to a large stone in the river, and said it was to be his gravestone. He died on 26 March 1945 with Frances holding one hand, his daughter Megan the other. The funeral was suitably simple, though the world took note of his departure and Churchill paid a tribute to him in the House of Commons which was far more eloquent and glowing than that which, soon afterward, he paid to Franklin D. Roosevelt.

Lloyd George will long be argued about; it is part of his charm that he is so open to criticism, so vulnerable to censure. He himself sought achievement and fame, but not apotheosis. He once said that he was not afraid of Hell, but would be terrified of going to Heaven. In my view, he was the most effective politician we have ever had, in peace as well as war. The problems that he had to tackle were quite unprecedented. Before him, no one had had to mobilise the resources of this country for a world war, nor had anyone had to face the social and economic consequences of such a war. It was largely thanks to him that Britain succumbed neither to military defeat nor to revolution; and if he had not been allowed to go to waste for two decades at the end of his life there is no telling what a difference he might not have made to our national fortunes.

His success owed much to the extraordinary way he had with people. He was intensely companionable, and he did not ration his high spirits according to the importance or otherwise of the people he happened to be with. He had all the egotism of the great, but in his case it was largely redeemed by good humour, gregariousness and a willingness to listen as well as talk. He did not behave like a self-conscious man of destiny and never put on the airs of a great statesman. Indeed, he debunked the whole idea of statesmanship by defining a statesman as simply 'a politician with whom one happens to agree'.

He was also very good at debunking other public figures. For instance, he said of Winston Churchill that 'he would make a drum out of the skin of his own mother in order to sound his own praises'. He made that comment though he was genuinely fond of Churchill. But he had no affection for Herbert Samuel, of whom he said that 'when they circumcised Herbert Samuel they threw away the wrong bit'. Lord Derby was a man whom he quite liked but did not admire. He said of Derby that he was 'like a cushion who always bore the impress of the last person who sat on him'. And he described Haig as 'brilliant to the top of his Army boots'. But by no means all his good remarks were personal. One of his best, which might almost be an epigram of Oscar Wilde, was this: 'The rich man can afford to be ignorant; the poor man can't'. His wit could express quite deep thoughts, though nearly always with a light touch.

At his burial place the big rough stone that he chose from the river is set in a rococo enclosure designed by Sir Clough Williams-Ellis (who also designed his memorial tablet in Westminster Abbey). The enclosure makes a superficially incongruous setting for the gravestone, but in reality the combination is appropriate, because Lloyd George was not just an elemental force from the Celtic twilight, as Keynes and others have suggested. He was quite as much, if not more, a rationalist in the eighteenth-century tradition. His second wife said of him that he was more like a Frenchman than a Welshman, and there is a good deal of truth in the remark. In any case it is surely beyond question that he was one of the most creative rulers Britain has ever had.

Lloyd George's last public appearance – and his first as Earl Lloyd George of Dwyfor – at a Criccieth Sunday School tea, 1 January 1945